Four Steps To Building A Profitable Coaching Practice

Four Steps To Building A Profitable Coaching Practice

A Complete Marketing Resource Guide for Coaches

Deborah Brown-Volkman

iUniverse, Inc.
New York Lincoln Shanghai

Four Steps To Building A Profitable Coaching Practice
A Complete Marketing Resource Guide for Coaches

iUniverse, Inc.

For information address:
iUniverse, Inc.
2021 Pine Lake Road, Suite 100
Lincoln, NE 68512
www.iuniverse.com

ISBN: 0-595-29660-2

Printed in the United States of America

This book is dedicated to Thomas J. Leonard, deceased, who was the founder and creator of the coaching profession. Thomas, thank you for giving me a career that brings me so much joy and satisfaction. I am forever indebted to your greatness and vision.

Introduction

This book is my story of how I grew a profitable coaching practice. I wrote this book so you could spend less time learning how to market your practice and have more time to grow it. In this book are the marketing tools and techniques I used to make coaching my full-time profession. Included are personal stories, examples, and copies of what I created to market and grow my practice.

I have created this book based on conversations I've had with hundreds of coaches, points I've learned from the amazing coach training programs in the marketplace today, and from my own experience. This book also taps into my 12 years of sales and marketing experience in the corporate world, and combines it with what I have learned since I began my practice.

I started coaching in August 1998. I completed my coach training at Coach U, and I coached clients in the evenings and weekends for three and a half years while I had a full-time job. I became a full-time coach in July 2001 after being laid off from a technology company.

I believe I have been a coach long before I officially joined the profession in 1998. Coaching was something I loved doing as far back as I can remember. (Do you feel this way too?) People were always coming to me for advice. I listened well. I encouraged them to GO FOR IT, take chances, and live their dreams. I loved being able to help others. I loved feeling appreciated. I loved that people respected my opinion and listened to my advice. Yet I never thought I could do this for a living.

In my eighth year working full-time in the corporate world, I was employed by a large global bank, and I was very unhappy. My job was crazy. I came into the office before the sun rose and left after the sun set. (Even in the summertime when the sun set later in the day, you could still find me at my desk.) I was getting paid a very good salary performing various marketing functions for the bank, yet I was unfulfilled. I remember one day putting my head in my hands and asking the universe for a way out. And there it was, in a Learning Annex catalog that came to my house a few days later. Included in the catalog was a seminar titled "How To Become A Personal Coach." I signed up, attended the seminar, and this was the day I realized I would be able to do what came naturally to me as a full-time profession.

The road to full-time coaching has not been an easy one. Fitting in classes, completing my coach training, and coaching clients while I had a full-time job was tough. Creating my marketing messages, selecting a target market, and creating a web site all took time. In addition, during the first three and a half years of my practice, I went back and forth internally. Can I really do this? What happens if I give someone the wrong advice? What happens if I am no good at this? But I plugged away because I felt like I was working towards my purpose in life.

My coaching practice was doing well, but did not take off until July of 2001 when I started coaching full-time. I remember sitting at my desk at home the day after I was laid off, wondering what I was going to do next. Even though there was information on how to coach, it was spread out all over the place. And there was no concrete information on how to make money at it. I said to myself that I was going to make it work, and then I was going to help other coaches do the same.

In my first year as full-time coach, I learned self-discipline, organization, and time management techniques. I taught myself HTML and updated my web site. I got focused, wrote articles like crazy, built a database of reporters for whom I could be an expert, started a coach chapter, and coached my heart out. I made sure I learned something new every day. And I worked with a coach who taught me how to sell, which was key to growing my practice.

All my hard work paid off. I now have a profitable coaching practice that continues to get bigger. And most importantly, I am fulfilling my life's purpose.

Whether you are a brand new coach and you are not sure how you will grow your practice, or you are an established coach who wants to learn the most you can about marketing so you can expand your practice, use this book to make your dream of becoming a profitable coach a reality.

How To Use This Book

The book is divided into the four steps I believe are necessary to create a profitable coaching practice. (There is also a bonus step on how to grow a profitable coaching practice using the press.) At the end of the book are resources you can use to implement the concepts discussed in each chapter. This book does not go into the specifics on how to start your practice, but how to grow it once you have it set up.

The beginning of the book begins with a section titled *The Importance of Marketing*. This section contains quotes from leaders in our profession on how key marketing is to growing your practice. Use their words of wisdom to inspire you to believe that making money as a coach and marketing your practice is possible.

Sprinkled throughout the chapters are a series of coaching assignments designed to make the marketing concepts clear. If you find that you are tempted to rush through these assignments or ignore them completely, please don't. They are an integral part of the book and process. Furthermore, they are at the heart of your experience of this book—one that will turn coaching into something which is both fulfilling and financially rewarding for you. Some assignments can be completed on the spot. Others you will have to think about or implement at a later time. If an assignment seems overwhelming, leave it, and come back to it later. It will be there when you are ready.

In addition, **DO NOT TRY TO IMPLEMENT EVERY CONCEPT AT ONCE.** When I started marketing my practice, I did one thing at a time. First, I started with a web site. Once that was done, I created an e-newsletter. Then I wrote articles. Then I got listed in search engines. Then I automated my practice. Then I created an e-book. Then I create an e-course. Once the on-line piece was completed, I created a coach chapter. Then I started working with the press. Then I started teaching teleclasses. Then I started speaking in front of live audiences. Then I started going to meetings where my target audience is located. Each was a separate project that I gave my full attention to until it was completed (or was up and running.) Then I moved onto something else. If you were building a house, you would not put up the roof until the foundation was done. Marketing works the same way.

To help you determine which concept to begin with, I have put an estimated time frame and cost to research each concept, get it up and running, and how long I believe it will take to make money from it. Use these as a guide and not as absolute numbers.

Complete step one and step two first, then move onto step three. Pick one concept in step three, develop it, get it up and running, and then move onto the next concept. This way you will not get overwhelmed. The goal is to build your practice in the order that is comfortable for you. There is no wrong or right way to do this. The pace and the timing are up to you.

Growing a profitable coaching practice takes hard work and patience. You will have moments of doubt and that is natural. You may wonder if you can learn what it takes to market yourself and your practice successfully. The answer is a resounding "YES!" You can. You simply have to do the work. Use this book to help you get there.

Table of Contents

Extended Contents: Where To Find What's Important To You

The Importance Of Marketing

While I'm known in the coaching business for attracting clients effortlessly, it doesn't mean that I don't market my practice. I just make sure that the marketing I do is fun! Every successful coach markets his or her services in one way or another, so keep experimenting until you find a way that works for you.

Talane Miedaner, Author of Coach Yourself to Success
Talane Coaching Company
http://www.lifecoach.com
talane@lifecoach.com
(407) 420-4042/1-888-4-Talane

Marketing is about being authentic. It's about making a connection and forming relationships that can transform lives. Some of the guiding principles of Coach U such as people have something in common, people want to contribute, people grow from connection, and people seek value, make this transformation happen. Marketing ties together these components, in a focused way, so you can convey your skills, talents, and abilities successfully to potential clients.

Sandy Vilas, MCC, CEO, CoachInc.com
1-800-48COACH (1-800-482-6224)
http://www.coachinc.com

Many coaches struggle with marketing because they don't know how to talk about what they do in a compelling way. Creating a memorable brand position, something that will have you stick out in the minds of potential clients, can solve this problem for you.

There are five key elements to every successful marketing strategy. They are:

- Having A Memorable You: This means getting crystal clear about how your values, experiences, knowledge, and quirks can be packaged for your ideal clients.
- Having Clarity: This means explaining what you do well.
- Having Authenticity: This means being real, which in turn, gets the attention of the people you want to work with.
- Having Consistency: This means presenting the same strong compelling message time after time.
- Having Intended Results: This means being polished and ready to share what you do with the world.

David Buck, President of CoachVille, LLC and the Schools of Coaching
http://www.coachville.com
http://www.davebuck.com

What is your marketing strategy? Do you know who your target audience is? Are you clear on the value you provide?

From thousands of hours of coaching business and professional individuals and groups, I have derived three key measurements called "The Three R's: Reach, Repetition, and Relevance." These are key to growing a profitable coaching practice. They are:

I. REACH: How many possible buyers/clients/customers/prospects know about your product or service?

II. REPETITION: How often do people in your potential market hear from you and your company?

III. RELEVANCE: Have you targeted your message to your best customers, and is it clear how you serve them and meet their needs?

Each of these measurements provides an opportunity for you to take action to improve your marketing efforts. Which measurement will you start with first? When will you begin? Get started and watch your practice grow.

Judy Feld, Master Certified Coach (MCC)
Certified Mentor Coach
President, International Coach Federation (ICF) 2003
judyfeld@coachnet.com
http://www.coachnet.com
972-931-6366

The difference between the average coaching practice and the extremely successful coaching practice can be summed up in one word…marketing. Many coaches believe they only need to be good at their craft. The fact is we are all business people first and coaches second. No matter how skillful or talented we may be, we will not enjoy a financially rewarding and fulfilling practice until we successfully promote our professional services.

Will Craig, MA, President, Coach Training Alliance and Past President, International Coach Federation-Denver
http://www.CoachTrainingAlliance.com
ideas@CoachTrainingAlliance.com
303-464-0110/888-432-4121

Many people ask me what it takes to have a successful business. The one thing I know (after starting six businesses and selling four of them) is that marketing is key. I've often said that you can be beat by someone with a lesser product or service if they market successfully and you don't. Never underestimate the necessity and value of marketing yourself.

Alicia Smith, DISC Ninja™
Coaching, Consulting & Training
http://www.discninja.com
http://www.disccertification.com
alicia@aliciasmith.com
406-994-9134

In the eight years that I have been an Executive Coach, I have noticed that only a small percentage of coaches earn a six-figure income. The difference between coaches who are successful and coaches who are struggling is marketing.

When I mentor new coaches, I often see coaches who are excellent at coaching but inexperienced as business people. It is important for a coach to make a decision: Is coaching my business? Or is it a hobby? If coaching is really a business for you, then having a strong marketing strategy is nonnegotiable.

The marketing techniques a coach chooses should match a coach's personal style. For example, since I coach senior corporate executives, I choose seminar and keynote speaking, writing books, and using the press. Those techniques worked for me because I found them easy and I enjoy being with corporate executives. However, other successful coaches I know have used e-newsletters, teleclasses, and networking to build their practices. The key is to select the marketing techniques that play to your particular strengths. They should be things you do naturally so marketing becomes part of your normal day. This is what makes marketing effortless and you successful.

Val Williams
Master Certified Coach
http://www.valwilliams.com
732-632-9647

So many coaches associate marketing with snake oil when, in fact, it's simply the way you present your services to your target audience as either the solution to a problem or a significant opportunity. That's all. Marketing ties all the pieces together in a cohesive and consistent fashion, including interaction with clients and prospects, the look of your promotional literature and packaging, your fees, policies, choices of venues, affiliations, and alliances. Ironically, it's the perception of marketing that stands in the way, not the art itself. If coaches can apply one of their own tools—shifting perspective—they'll discover the use of marketing can be a powerful and personalized ally in their road to success.

Andrea Feinberg
President, Coaching Insight
Vice President, United Coaching Associates
http://www.coachinginsight.com
http://www.unitedcoachingassociates.com
andrea@coachinginsight.com
516-338-6842

Marketing is not only important, it's vital to growing a solid coaching practice. And even though it takes time to build a profitable practice, with patience and persistence, it can be done. So what holds many coaches back? Two things: the first is not having an effective marketing campaign, and the second is not having a system to follow up on prospective clients. There is nothing worse than spending money on a marketing campaign that is not successful because you did not have a good system in place to handle leads and new clients. You want to make sure that your hard work and effort do not fall through the cracks.

Sylva K. Leduc, M.Ed., MPEC
Certified Executive Coach
President, Client Compass
http://www.ClientCompass.com

Marketing helps you connect and stay connected with current and new clients. Be seen as the expert in your field and give something away that is useful to the world.

Michael Losier
Vice President, TeleClass International Services, Inc.
http://www.TeleClassInternational.com
michael@michaellosier.com
877-550-9282/250-380-9282

You can create the best cake if you use the right ingredients and follow the best recipe. You can have a prospering practice if you have the right marketing program. Marketing is the ingredient that will make it happen.

Brigitte Nadeau
CEO and Founder, Audio Strategies
http://www.AudioStrategies.com
brigitte@audiostrategies.com

Coaches need marketing just as plants need water. It is literally the lifeblood of your practice. Being skillful at your craft is a great idea, but without marketing, you'll have very little opportunity to exercise that skill or expand it. Imagine your practice with many one-on-one customers, several paid teleclasses, and an e-book or e-zine bringing in income. Imagine your bank account getting larger each day. Being a profitable coach is possible if you want it.

Craig Jennings
Professional Coach & President of the NYC Midtown Coaching Center
http://www.nycmcc.com
http://www.craigjennings.com
craig@craigjennings.com
516-944-6454

Live a great life. This is the beginning of marketing yourself as a coach. Design a game this year. Offer your coaching services to one hundred people free of charge. Follow-up with a telephone call mentioning something you remember that was of value to the client. Have no attachment. This is the beginning of a full practice.

Katherine Gotshall English
Life Coach
kathcoach@earthlink.net
212-529-8512

Like many professions, coaching is a relationship-driven business. We must be authentic, credible, focused and crystal clear about who we are, who we coach best, and how we provide value. There is still some educating to do to get the word out there about how great coaching truly is. So many coaches get stuck on marketing. The good news is you can make improvements as you grow wiser over time.

Jonathan Flaks, PCC
Professional Certified Coach
President, Jonathan Flaks Coaching Associates, Inc.
Founder and Past President, Westchester County (NY) International Coach Federation (ICF) Chapter
877-700-BOLD/914-479-0568
http://www.jfcoach.com
jonathan@jfcoach.com

Anyone who' has dared to take a bold, new step and engage in the exciting adventure that is starting your own practice will learn that the old adage "if you build it, they will come" is just that—an old adage. How many web sites sit on that Internet highway, barely getting noticed as we whiz by on our way to some other site with flashing neon signs and promises of the world for free? As coaches, we have a wild passion for helping others and boundless enthusiasm for finally having found the thing we were most born to do. Get your passionate message out to the world so others will know you exist.

Susan Eckert, MA, CCM
Career Coach
Principal, Advance Career & Professional Development
http://www.advancecareerdevelopment.com
susan@advancecareerdevelopment.com
800-824-6611/631-666-3224

Marketing is a plan, an analysis of your clients, your competition and an understanding of how your services fit into the overall picture. Marketing goes beyond "getting the word out." It is a client-centered approach that allows you to focus your energies and resources on incorporating initiatives that draws clients into your practice.

Linda Matias, JCTC, CEIP
Career Coaching and Outplacement Services
President, CareerStrides
34 East Main Street #276
Smithtown, NY 11787
http://www.careerstrides.com
631-382-2425

Marketing is a scary word for many coaches. A lot of us, for one reason or another, would rather not call attention to ourselves in "too loud" a way. But you need to market your practice in order to survive. So the question lies—where, when, and how to begin?

You might think to yourself, "If only I can get recognized solely on the merits of doing what I do and doing it well. Why can't I just build my business strictly through referrals?" That would be in a perfect world. Or would it really? Much to my own delight, I have found that every time I rise to the occasion, write copy for my new brochure, update my web site, fulfill a request by an organization to give a presentation, show up at a networking meeting, or get even the smallest quote published, I redefine and sharpen my mission. The sheer exercise of it serves to help me get clear on what it is I do for my clients, thereby making the breadth, quality and value of my work that much more powerful for existing and potential clients.

Don't be the world's best-kept secret. (That won't serve anyone.) Toot your own whistle and ring your own bell. Trust me, other people will join in.

Rachel B. Spaulding
Public Speaking, Presentation, and Communications Skills Coach
Ovations By Design
A Division of Dream It Design It Live It
http://www.live-it-coach.com
Rachel@live-it-coach.com
718-275-2074

The Foundation For Becoming A Profitable Coach

Here are some tips before we begin. They are your foundation for becoming a profitable coach.

- Be clear on who you coach and what you offer potential clients. Don't let people guess what you do.

- Be passionate. Your excitement for what you do needs to come across in your marketing efforts. Many people do not have lives or careers that fulfill them. This is why they are coming to you. If you have passion, they will want it too. What prospective clients are buying is you.

- Be yourself. No one does what you do better than you. Never forget that you have a unique gift to give to the world.

- Stay positive. Read motivational books or articles. Listen to motivational tapes. Stay away from bad news on a regular basis. There is a difference between catching up versus being weighed down by current events.

- Get coach training and attend coaching conferences. Know the basics and what you are doing. This will increase your confidence and make marketing easier.

- Always be on the lookout for new ideas. This will keep your creative juices flowing and invigorate you.

- Get known. Use the marketing technique in this book so people have a sense of who you are before they meet you. Focus in on what makes you different. Provide value that others do not. Become an expert. Your knowledge will impress potential clients.

- Have clear goals. It does not matter how many other coaches there are in the marketplace. What do you want? What do you provide? What do you want your coaching practice to look like? Do you want to work every day or only three days a week? How many clients do you want to work with? How much money do you want to make? Will your coaching practice consist of one-on-one coaching or will it be filled with e-coaching or coaching groups? Where will you be six months from now, one year, and longer? Get this down on paper. Put it into a plan. Look at your plan every day. Make it a part of your life.

• Get a mentor coach. Look for someone who has done what you want to do. You don't have to have this instant, all encompassing connection with your coach the first time you speak to him or her. Did you feel this way when you first met your lawyer or accountant? Yes, a connection is important, but sometimes the universe sends us different types of people so we can learn from them. Hire someone who is successfully doing what you want to do. Hire someone to whom you can say, "I want what you have." If you want a full-time coaching practice, make sure your coach is coaching full time.

• Do what you say you will do. If you promise someone something, send it right away. If you cannot do it, say this upfront. If you cannot keep your promise, tell the person immediately, and provide a new date when they can expect what you promised. All you have as a coach is your word. Do not underestimate its power to make or break your practice.

Step 1: Decide Who You Want To Coach

Estimated Time To Figure Out: 30 To 180 Days

Approximate Cost: Your Time

Specialization brings profits. Diversification brings confusion.

Many coaches are afraid to pick who they want to coach. They worry that they are walking away from something, such as a missed opportunity or potential clients. They worry that they are being too narrow or limiting by specializing. What you really walk away from is an unproductive strategy. You cannot coach the whole world successfully.

What you walk towards is something much greater—coaching the kind of clients you understand well. The reward for your more defined choice is direction and focus, two key elements that will transform your practice and your life.

When you start coaching, it may seem like a daunting task to decide who you want to coach. And if you have been coaching for a while, it still may be difficultt to choose. There are so many possibilities and you want to revel in all of them. My suggestion is that you do. Try them all on and see which one(s) feel best. Then make your choice, so you can have focus and direction.

How do you choose who you want to coach? Start by thinking about the type of people who you naturally attract into your life. Who have you helped, who do you enjoy helping, and who do you want to help? The answers will help you come up with a clear description.

The Selection Process

The easiest way to determine who you will coach is by taking out a piece of paper and drawing three vertical lines, creating four columns. Title the page "Who I Have Helped." In the first column list every person you have helped (yes, everyone), whether it is someone who was in your personal or business life. In the second column list the specific problems they had. In the third column list the action you took to help them. In the last column list what they accomplished as a result of your suggestions, coaching, or advice.

Here are some examples:

Who I Have Helped			
Person's Name	Problem	Action	Accomplishment
Bob	Getting beaten up in grade school.	Taught him how to stand up for himself.	Spoke back to the boys who were giving him trouble. As a result, they left him alone.
Sue	Didn't get along with one of her teachers in college.	Helped her come up with a plan to make things smoother at school.	She got an 'A' that semester.
Linda	Difficulty with coworker.	Encouraged her to speak with coworker even thought she was afraid to do so.	Linda spoke with her coworker and they worked things out. They have not had difficulties since.

When you complete this exercise you will notice that there is a pattern. Are there more men or women listed in the columns? Are they younger or older? Are they concerned about their health, relationships, or career?

In this example, you can see that this coach has naturally been able to help others to communicate better. Possibly this coach would assist others on "How To Get Along With Difficult Coworkers." Or teachers. Or friends, family, etc. You could build an entire practice solely on how to communicate effectively.

Note: this is a tough exercise, but one that is very important to go through and complete. Many coaches have said to me that they do not remember whom they have helped, or cannot find a pattern. Take your time. Spend as much as you need thinking about how to complete this grid. Ask the people in your life and your coach for feedback. Do not give up. You can do this.

Here's a real life example:

Lisa (not her real name) was a client of mine from California. She was a successful entrepreneur in other businesses she owned, but her coaching practice was not growing as quickly as she would have liked. During our initial conversation, I discovered that Lisa had not selected a specific group of people to coach. I asked Lisa do the grid exercise, and this is what she came up with:

- More women than men asked for her opinion
- She helped a lot of women either start or grow their business
- She helped women who were leaders in their respective fields
- She helped women who were happy in their relationships

After completing this exercise, Lisa realized that her target audience (a marketing term that refers to the group she would be coaching) was women leaders who were secure in their relationships, and either wanted to start a business or expand the business they had, traits very similar to her own. Once Lisa achieved clarity, the rest was implementation. She refocused all her marketing efforts to attract her targeted group. As a result, Lisa signed up three new clients within a month.

Coaching Assignment #1:

Complete this grid: (Use a separate piece of paper if you need more space.)

Who I Have Helped			
Person's Name	Problem	Action	Accomplishment

Do you see similarities in the people you have helped? Is it becoming clear whom you would coach?

Who You Coach Is You

Let me explain this further. When I first started coaching, I was a personal coach. I helped people live their dreams. I marketed my practice in the beginning through writing. I started an e-newsletter that went from eighteen people I knew and grew to thousands of subscribers within a few years. My subscribers loved what I wrote. They sent me thank you e-mails and letters, but they were not buying my coaching services. I believe it was because I was not clear about whom I wanted to coached. Although I was clear that I wanted to help people live better lives, I was not clear about who those people were.

The second phase of building my practice was to get clear on whom I coached. I dropped the personal coach and became a career coach. I went from "You Can Have A Life You Love" to "You Can Have A Career You Love." This was a good focus for me because I had switched jobs every couple of years when I was in the corporate world (because I was so unhappy). I had experience with writing cover letters, editing resumes, interviewing techniques, and salary negotiations. As a result of my new focus, I got a few more clients. Still, my practice was growing very slowly.

Out of sheer determination to find out why people were not buying my coaching services, I started a Research and Development team (a group of people who were loyal e-newsletter subscribers), and asked them what was missing from my web site and my services. They said that I was all over the place. At that time, I was helping the following with their careers:

- Entrepreneurs
- Small Business Owners
- Professionals
- Doctors
- Lawyers
- Executives
- Students
- And anyone else who had a career issue!

It was too much. My Research and Development team said they did not feel like I was coaching them; rather that I was coaching everyone. They said they felt as if I did not understand them. Therefore, as a result, they wouldn't hire me. These were tough comments to hear because I had spent so much time getting my practice to this point that the thought of making another change was discouraging. But I asked for the truth because I wanted to hear it. I was still very determined to grow my practice and, if it took tweaking my messages further, that's what I would do.

I took what they said to heart and did something about it. I looked inward. I asked myself, "Who am I and what can I give back to the world?"

My background was in the corporate world, in management, and I understood what management goes through. I started as a worker and left creating strategic plans and leading teams. I knew what it was like to work smart, not hard, because I was building a coaching practice while working full-time. I had to learn how to be efficient because (after 5 p.m.) I had clients to coach and classes to take. I learned time management techniques—prioritizing and scheduling. In addition, I had left the corporate world to start my own business, not any business, but a business I loved. I could help other corporate executives do the same. Thus, my target market was born. I started coaching senior executives, vice presidents, and managers. I updated my web site and changed my services so they were geared towards this audience exclusively.

Giving Back

USH BUT I SEE THE ADVANTAGE OF COACHING FROM YOUR EXPERIENCE

I believe that coaching is about teaching what you know. Not everyone agrees with my philosophy, and that's ok. But I get a lot of questions from new and established coaches that want to know how I got my practice to where it is today. I tell them that the teaching aspect is an important component.

What can you teach? I suggest that you stand in one place, turn around, and look. Your target group in all likelihood will be the people behind you who want to be where you are today. It does not matter what you haven't learned yet. Focus on those who want to learn what you already know.

Here are examples from coaches who used the concept of giving back when they selected whom to coach:

"I was a business owner, so I will coach business owners on how to handle the stress of running a business and managing employees to be their best."

"I survived a tragic accident and lived to tell about it. I will teach others how to do the same."

"I left the corporate world and started my own business. I've never been happier. I will coach executives who want this happiness too."

"I have been married to my husband for 30 years. I will coach couples to build a solid relationship like my husband and I have."

Note: There are other ways to choose whom you will coach. Some coaches see an opportunity or an unfulfilled need in the marketplace and start a coaching practice based on that. Either way, be very clear about who your clients are. Clarity makes building your practice easier.

Coaching Assignment #2

Make a list of all the experiences you have had in your life. Make another list of the things you want to teach and give back to the world. Write until you cannot think of another thing to add. Then, come back in a day or two and add more.

Use what you learned in Assignments #1 and #2 to decide whom you will coach. (This will become your target audience. You will know when you have it when you are able to say it in one sentence.) If you are not sure which group to choose, keep working on the exercises until you are. Ask your coach to help you.

You can choose a few different groups or just one group to coach, but make a choice. You may be right or you may be wrong in your choice, but give yourself credit for making a decision. If you need to feel more comfortable with your choice, put a time frame on it—say, six months—to see how it goes. If something does not feel right to you, trust your intuition. Either tweak your choice it or go through the process again. I promise that your time will not be wasted. If you go with your heart, and what feels right to you, your choice will be the winner.

Coaching Assignment #3

Do research. Go on the coach referral sites and check out what other coaches are doing. Check out anywhere from 50 to 100 web sites. Go on non-coach related sites and see what these companies or people are doing. Put in the keywords associated with the target audience you have chosen, such as career, relationships, communication, etc. Your goal is to get a sense of who is out there and what they are doing so you can see what distinguishes you from the rest. You also want to make sure there is a market for your services.

Note: If you find that you've gone through the book to this point without doing the exercises, consider how much you really want this or if this is the right time to build your practice. Ask yourself if you are willing to the undergo self-examination and do the work. Ask yourself if you are willing to move past obstacles, uncertainty, or fear. If the answer is "No," or "I'm really too busy right now to do these exercises," or "I'm not ready," then you've made an important discovery.

Stop and ask yourself, "Do I really want a profitable coaching practice now?" (Choosing the right time to grow a coaching practice is important.) Whatever your answer, it is fine. But know that your answer makes a difference. The coaches who tell me, "I want this!" have a greater chance of getting a profitable practice quicker than those who say, "I will be a coach someday." I am not saying that the second group will not be successful. I am saying that it will take them longer to grow their practice.

If you need more time, use the book to get comfortable with the different aspects of marketing and think about how you will market your practice in the future. When you are done, put this book in a place where you can find it when you are ready.

Step 2: Create A Program Your Target Audience Will Pay You For

Estimated Time To Create: 30 To 90 Days

Approximate Cost: Your Time If You Create Your Own. $100 To $5,000 If You Purchase Someone Else's.

Once you have a target audience, it is time to develop a program that will easily explain what you do and what's included in your coaching fee.

Before I had a program, when a prospective client asked me how I would coach them, I explained that my process consisted of asking open-ended questions, role-playing, and giving them assignments to work on during the week. To me, this made perfect sense. I knew the process best. I was the coach. But I was not disclosing the process in a way that had prospective clients saying "I want more!" (I believe at the time I did not disclose it because I did not know what it was fully. I had an idea what it was, but really it was a "we will see how it develops process.") I felt confident that there was a method to my madness and the client would get results. It just wasn't something I could spell out clearly in the beginning because it would be revealed over time during our coaching sessions.

Unfortunately, this was not concrete enough. Potential clients wanted to understand and be able to visualize in their minds what they were getting for their coaching fee. Even though they partially understood what I was saying, and they thanked me for my time, the number of clients I coached grew slowly.

Mapping Out A Program

I decided to map out what I do. I developed a five-step program that takes clients from point A to point B, identifying their problems, and coming up with a process for solving them. Once I had a program, something tangible that people could grasp, my practice really took off.

Here is my 5-step program:

1. **D** escribe what you want
2. **E** xplore your options
3. **C** reate your game plan
4. **I** mplement your plan
5. **R** each your goal

The concept behind my program is simple. It is based on the premise that if you can get clear on what you want, the rest is implementation. It was the process I had used all along, but now it was concrete.

This is how I explained it. I will help you get clear on what you want (The DESCRIBE phase), and then I will direct you through the research process so you can see if what you want is doable or not (The EXPLORE phase). We will also get all of your unanswered questions answered so you can make a decision about what to do next in your career. Next, I will help you create and implement a workable and realistic plan (The GAME PLAN phase). The plan will be very specific and will include a roadmap for its completion. Finally, I will help you reach your goal (The IMPLEMENT phase). I will be your support, someone to brainstorm with, and will hold you accountable to the promises you make to me each week. I will also celebrate with you, encourage you to enjoy your accomplishment, and then challenge you to take on bigger goals in the future (The REACH YOUR GOAL phase).

I was amazed by the response I was getting when I explained this to potential clients, especially on complimentary calls. Potential clients liked what I was saying and they were paying me to have access to it. This increased my confidence tremendously because I was getting paid more as a coach, and I had people who were agreeing and getting on board with a program I believed in.

Coaching Tip: Some clients may start your program at step one. Others will join at a later step. In my five-step program, clients may know what they want, but not know how to get there. If this is the case, we would skip step number one, which is defining what they want, and go right into step number two, which is researching their alternatives so they can make a decision about which direction to go next. Some clients have completed step one and two on their own, and want a coach who will hold them accountable for creating and implementing a plan to reach their goal. It does not matter where a client begins. What's key is that you have a program that spells out the process you will use to help them get results.

Client Example

Nancy (not her real name) is a client of mine. After I walked Nancy though the process of choosing whom to coach, she was ready to create her program. Nancy is a coach who works with executives in large corporations. Her focus is on helping them restore safety and trust in their divisions. Massive layoffs that occurred as a result of a down economy have left employees mistrustful of their bosses and of how their companies are being run. Nancy wanted to create a program that showcased her professionalism and her coaching skills. This is what we came up with:

TRUST: 5 STEPS TO A SAFER AND MORE PRODUCTIVE WORK ENVIRONMENT

T eamwork
R ecognition
U nity
S afety
T rust

Here is how Nancy uses her TRUST program specifically:

TEAMWORK: Identify the executive's working relationship with senior management, direct reports, and subordinates. Uncover what's not working. Evaluate the executive's strengths, weaknesses, and communication style. Assessments may or may not be used at this stage.

RECOGNITION: Work with the executive to recognize those individuals who have contributed to the organization. Trust and teamwork is in the early stages of being restored.

UNITY: Work with the executive to utilize these individuals as a resource to help create a new vision for the division. Map out how this vision will increase morale, productivity, and trust going forward. Vision will be tied into the organization's goals.

SAFETY: Work with the executive to implement this vision, creating a roadmap for its execution. Included will be team accountability and how the team will contribute to the result. Work with the executive to encourage contributions, allow participation, and trust workers more.

TRUST: Work with the executive so he/she can reacclimatize the division to the new way of doing business. In this stage, trust is restored, and the executive can switch to being proactive instead of reactive. Thought processes and working habits are shifted so the executive can work less and inspire more.

Nancy told me recently that having this program makes potential clients feel more comfortable hiring her. In addition, she is more confident speaking with potential clients because she has something concrete to offer.

Note: You do not need an acronym to have a successful program. As long as the steps are mapped out and in sequential order, your program IS the number of steps it takes to achieve the results your target audience is seeking. Nancy could eliminate the acronym altogether and let potential clients know that she has a five-step program to create a trusted and more productive work environment. She chose the acronym because she was looking for something catchy.

Finding Problems To Solve

All successful programs help solve a problem. Weight WatchersÔ programs help you lose weight so you can feel better about yourself. Coaching schools solve the problem of providing training so you can start your own business or work in a career that gives you purpose and meaning. My DECIR™ program helps solve the problem of those who are out of work or overworked so you don't have to dread the thoughts of work anymore.

If we go back to Nancy, she knew that executives were spending too much time trying to reassure employees that everything was going to be okay. In addition, she knew that executives were tired, and getting burnt out because these conversations were preventing them from getting their work done. She built these problems into her program and this is why it was successful.

Your program will not be successful unless it solves a problem. This is because potential clients do not buy until they have a problem they need to solve, and they have exhausted all possibilities of solving the problem(s) themselves. One of the biggest frustrations I hear from coaches is that potential clients tell them that they need time to "think it over" when the question of "Will you hire me?" comes up. This is because the coach has probably not zeroed in on what their target markets' problems are, and as a result, potential clients do not have a compelling reason to hire them at that moment. Potential clients buy when they are in trouble or need something they cannot get on their own.

Note: Problems change over time. The problems I presently help senior executives, vice presidents, and managers solve are how to get a job when you have been out of work for awhile, or how to deal with a large workload if you are still working. As the economy improves, I will focus on helping senior executives, vice presidents, and managers get back on track and readjust to working life again, or how to be proactive instead of reactive when more resources are available. Your target market, in most instances, stays the same. The problems they need help solving change as the circumstances around them alters.

What problems do most people need help solving? Here are a few ideas:

- How to make more money/become financially independent
- How to find a soul mate/have great relationships
- How to have friends/be socially accepted
- How to gain recognition, power, and acceptance
- How to be heard/understood
- How to have a career that has meaning and purpose
- How to lose weight/be healthy
- How to have balance and be stress free

these are on the wheel

Coaching Assignment #4

Get clear on the specific problems your target audience is facing. List every single conceivable problem that you believe your target audience is having. When you are tired of writing, take a break, and then write some more. Put yourself in their shoes; what are they feeling, experiencing, going through, etc. Then, start talking to people who are members of your target audience and find out if they agree or disagree with this list, and what you should add/delete to make it complete.

Complete this grid. (Use a separate piece of paper if you need more space.)

Target Audience (Use definition from Coaching Assignment #2)
Problems

Coaching Assignment #5

Create a program for your target audience. List all the steps you would walk a client through to help them solve their problems—list everything you can think of. The list does not have to be in any particular order initially. Then, put the steps into sequential order. Try to keep the list between three to six steps. This will be your program. Create an acronym or leave it as it.

Next, begin documenting how your program works. Are there checklists or forms you need to create? Are there assessments that you can either pay for or use from your coach training tuition? Are there workbooks, special reports, or questionnaires you can include? Potential clients like to see written materials. Include what is available or create your own. (Use the resources at the back of this book to assist you.)

Deciding What To Charge For Your Program

Today (at the book's print date), most coaching is done by telephone. (The rest is done in person and by e-mail.) Coaching is sold in monthly increments. The number of times per month you speak with and spend on the phone with clients can vary between 3 and 4 times a month, 30 minutes to one hour per call. I like to coach clients 3 times a month, 50 minutes per call. This schedule is what I am most comfortable with. Even though my policy is to coach clients 3 times a month, if I get the feeling that clients need more assistance (especially in the first month), I will ask them if they would like a fourth call as a bonus. I offer unlimited e-mail support because I have found that the clients who do the best are the ones I communicate with during the week. I also have created a client-only resource page on my web site that is filled with resources I have been collecting since 1998. It provides motivation, assistance, and information my clients can use between calls. Access is included in the monthly coaching fee.

Coaching involves commitment and the promise that a client will work with you over time, which sets the coaching relationship in the right direction. Clients can hire me for six months, three months, or for a one-month trial period. My one-month program is more expensive on a per month basis than my six-month program. I do this because the longer I work with a client, the better I get to know them. This knowledge accelerates their progress. In addition, one month is seldom enough time to help clients reach their goals. In most cases, you first have to help them clear things out of the way before they can start working on their goals. This does not mean that your clients have to work with you forever. It does mean that there are no quick fixes in life and this applies to coaching as well.

Here's a formula that will help you determine what to charge:

1. **Determine** how much money you want and/or need to make over the course of a year. Add up all of your yearly expenses plus the amount you want to have in savings. Add 50% to this number to cover taxes and health insurance. This is your yearly income goal. Take this number and divide it by 12. This is your monthly income goal.

Example: $100,000 (which is the total of your expenses, savings/profit, and additional money to cover taxes and insurance) divided by 12 (for 12 months) is $8,333 per month.

2. **Determine** how many hours each month you have to coach. Subtract the hours you need to run and market your practice. (You want to know the amount of time you have available to actually coach.) Divide this number by four, representing each week per month.

Example: You have 160 hours each month for coaching. If you need 80 hours for marketing, and 40 hours to handle administrative matters, then you have 40 hours left for pure coaching. When you divide this number by four, you have 10 hours per week to coach clients.

3. **Determine** how many clients you want to work with each month.

Example: If you work with one client each hour, once a week, using the calculation in #2 above, you can work with 10 clients per month. If you coach clients 3 times a month, then you can use the 4th week to work on your coaching practice or take time off.

4. **Divide** your calculation in #1 by your calculation in #3.

Example: $8,333 divided by 10 clients is $833. This is your monthly rate per client if you coach 10 clients once a week per month.

This monthly fee for your coaching program will change depending on the amount of money you want to make and the number of hours you have available to coach. If you want to charge a lower monthly coaching fee, and you still want to make $100,000, reduce both the amount of money you charge each client AND the time you spend with them, so you can increase the number of clients you work with. You may even consider putting clients into coaching groups so you can work with even more clients at one time.

This fee calculation is for telephone coaching. Your rate for visiting clients will be higher. You will need to factor in the time and expense to get there. Or if you have a location where clients come to you, you'll have expenses such as rent, etc. In addition, there is more cost for paper for in person coaching. If you are coaching by telephone, e-mail attachments will suffice. In person, you will need to incur the expense of creating, copying, and putting together documents that you and your clients can work on together, or for them to take away as weekly assignments.

> **Coaching Tip:** Coaching is about expanding our clients and ourselves. Money is a touchy topic. If you want to expand as a coach, charge a fee that is slightly above what feels comfortable. You will grow into it.

Coaching Assignment #6

Create your fee structure. Think about whether you will be doing in person coaching, telephone coaching, e-mail coaching, or group coaching. Set up different rates for each type of service, and vary the rate based on how long clients sign up. Use the fee formula to assist you and pick a fee structure that you are comfortable with. Then, when a potential client asks how much you charge, you can tell them what you charge with clarity and confidence.

Step 3: Create A Marketing Strategy

Once you know who want to coach and what services you offer, it's time to tell the world that you are open for business.

Here's some insight into marketing. Marketing is simple. Marketing is straight-forward. You do one thing, and you get another. For example, you put up a web site, and people visit it. You write an e-newsletter, and people read it. You speak to a local business group, and people listen to what you have to say. The confusion comes in when you are trying to figure out which thing to do first, or you are trying to do everything at once.

If you are struggling with marketing, know that you are not alone. As a few coaches recently said to me:

"I need feedback and tips on how to market my coaching practice. This has been my biggest hurdle so far."

"Marketing seems so hard and overwhelming."

"I don't know where to start."

"I don't like marketing and don't want to do it."

Marketing is about showing up on a consistent basis. Many coaches say to me, "I love what you are doing!" or "I see your name everywhere! How do you do it?" There is no secret. It's because I show up. I market myself regularly. I use the basic principle of coaching, which is "It's not the one thing you do, but the one thing you do over time."

The Three Main Ways To Market Your Coaching Practice

There are three ways to market your coaching practice. I break them down into three categories: writing, speaking, and networking.

Each category has several concepts. For each concept, write down your goals. If you are developing a web site, what do you want it to accomplish? Do you want it to be informative so people can call you to find out more (some coaches use their web site solely for the purpose of having people call them for complimentary calls), or do you want it to be filled with e-products that people can buy from your site directly? If you are writing an e-newsletter, will it go out monthly or quarterly? If you are writing articles, how many will you send out each year, and when specifically will they go out? If you want to grow your practice using speaking, how many presentations will you give each year? If you want to grow your practice using networking, how many meetings will you attend each year? Write this down. Put your strategy into your calendar. This will be your game plan.

So which concept do you begin with? Start with the one you enjoy the most. If you enjoy writing, create a web site or write an article to market your coaching practice.

If you like to speak in front of people, speak at a local association or organization in your neighborhood. Get known and then move onto other and larger venues.

If you like to talk with people, start with networking. Select a few associations or chamber of commerce meetings. Go to these meetings on a regular basis. Volunteer your time. This is how people will get to know you.

Coaching Tip: Pick one concept, develop it, get it up and running, and then move onto the next. This way you will not get overwhelmed.

3-1: Writing As A Marketing Strategy

Writing can take on many different shapes. It can be an e-newsletter, a special report, or an article that gets published or picked up by the media. Surpass Your Dreams, my e-newsletter, was started in 1999 with 18 subscribers, all people I knew personally. Today, it has a global subscriber base of over 13,000, and has generated a steady stream of clients. I converted it to a paid subscription in 2001 and am making passive revenue from it. I have also been asked to be a career expert by many reporters and journalists after they found an article I wrote on-line. (Note: Don't forget to add a copyright notice to your work. You do not want anyone to steal or reuse your words.)

What follows are some ways you can grow your practice with your written words:

A. Creating A Web Site

Estimated Time To Get It Up And Running: 90 To 180 Days

Estimated Time To Make Money From It: 180 To 360 Days

Approximate Cost: $100 For A Web Template To $3,000 For A Web Designer. $25 to $75 Per Month For Web Hosting.

Many coaches ask me if they should have a web site. My answer is yes. Why not have a vehicle that is open for business 24 hours a day, 7 days a week worldwide? Still, it is not essential to have a web site to successfully market your coaching practice. Many coaches have used the speaking and networking concepts solely in this book to successfully grow their coaching practices. If you decide to go forward with a web site, here are some tips to get it up and running. If you prefer to wait, then skip this section, and come back to it at a later time.

1. Why A Web Site?

A web site gives you instant credibility. People get to know you and when they contact you, they are a much more qualified group to discuss coaching with because they have already looked at your site, your program, your fees, etc. They already have a sense of who you are, and they like what they have read so far. As a coach, you are selling a service that people cannot see or touch. Your web site makes you and your practice seem real.

The content you will create for your web site can be the foundation to prepare all of your other marketing materials. A web site forces you to think about what you offer and how to say it well. Once you have this wording, it can be used for brochures, speaking outlines, e-newsletters, articles, one-sheeters, e-books, etc.

2. Who Designs It?

Good question. It depends on whether you want to control the addition of new content or not. If you know the web well and are comfortable with it, pick up the latest web design tools and design it yourself. If you do not, or do not have a family member or friend who can design a web site for you, consider hiring a professional designer. (The work you did previously searching other coaches' web sites will come in handy when describing to a family member or designer how you would like your site to look.) If you go down the path of choosing a designer, you can request that they design it, and then show you how to make future changes yourself. This will be very helpful if you make a lot of changes to your web site as I do. It will also keep your web costs down, as having a designer make changes to your web site can be expensive.

If you select a designer, most can register your domain name and host the web site for you. This is a nice added service. If not, search on the web for "domain name registration" and "web hosting" and do this yourself.

If You Are Working With A Designer, Be Prepared To Tell Them The Following:

- Your experience with web sites. It is important that they know how much you know and don't know. (Do not worry. They will not hold this against you.)
- Your intent. Do you want to sell or just convey information?
- The content you will be using.
- How long you want your web site to be. (Example: A few pages or many.)

- Any special design or logo you would like to use. (Note: lots of large graphics will take longer to load. If your web site takes awhile to load, visitors will not stick around.)
- The type of style you like. (Example: do you want to be business like or more informal?)
- What automation you would like to add initially or down the road.

You Will Also Want To Know: (Get this in writing.)

- How much the web site will cost, what is included (and not included), and how many revisions you get before there are additional charges.
- How long it will take to create the web site.
- What updates will cost if you decide to outsource web site changes and how long they take.
- Can they offer a process whereby you can make simple updates of your website without fuss or cost?
- Do they understand the latest technology? Can they help you with this or do you have to do the legwork on your own?
- What other web sites they have designed. Check them out. If you do not like their work, you probably will not like the site they design for you either.
- Will your web site load quickly and look good on different types of computers and browsers?

3. Web Site Content Outline

Below is an outline you can use to create the content for your web site. You do not have to fill in every section. Your web site will be ever changing and growing.

I. Home Page The home page is the most important page. It has to stand out and get the readers' attention. If visitors like your home page, they will click on other pages.

1. List the major points about your practice that you want people to know. Include questions that will pique the reader's interest. Make the home page interesting and motivational. People who visit your site are there because they want to make changes in their lives.

2. List your bio
3. Your contact information
4. Get a picture of yourself to put on your site

II. What Is Coaching? (optional)

1. Describe what coaching is in your opinion
2. Frequently Asked Questions (FAQs) and Answers
3. Add anything else that you want the reader to know about coaching
4. Your contact information

III. How a Coach Can Help You/Programs You Offer

1. Explain how a coach can help the reader
2. List your program and the benefits to the reader
3. Add anything else you would like the reader to know about how your program(s) can help them
4. Your contact information

IV. Assessments (if applicable)

1. List assessments or tests that you would like to include on your site
2. Your contact information

V. 10 Reasons to Hire A Coach (or other top ten's or articles you want the reader to see.)

1. You can get these from www.topten.org or by doing a search on the web. Do not forget to get permission from the author to do so.
2. Your contact information

VI. Testimonials

1. List testimonials you've received from clients
2. Your contact information

VII. Seminars & Workshops (if applicable)

1. List seminars, workshops, or teleclasses you are giving
2. Your contact information

VIII. Media Relations (if applicable)

1. List press releases or stories written or quoted by you
2. Your contact information

IX. Fees

1. List fees
2. List type of payments you accept
3. Shopping cart/e-commerce system
4. Your contact information

X. Resource Page/Links

1. List links to resources you believe will benefit your visitors
2. Your contact information

XI. Newsletter Archive Page (if applicable)

1. List issues of newsletters you have written
2. Your contact information

XII. Article Archive Page (if applicable)

1. List titles of articles you have written
2. Your contact information

XIII. Products

1. List books, e-courses, cassettes, CDs, or e-books that you are selling
2. Your contact information

Note: Many coaches ask me if they should put their fees on their web site. My answer is yes. It screens those who cannot afford your coaching services. This is a good thing. This means you will spend less time having conversations about your coaching program(s) with the wrong people and have more time to attract the right people. In addition, buyers feel more comfortable knowing what the price is. They are accustomed to it. When you walk into a grocery or a department store, the prices are already on the goods. Imagine how frustrating it would be to have to walk up to the cashier or a sales clerk to get a price every time you want to find out what an item costs. Make it easy for potential clients to decide if your fee is in their price range before they contact you. They will appreciate it.

Coaching Assignment #7

Decide if you will be creating a web site. If you are, select a domain name and register it. Go onto the coach referral web sites (do a search on the internet under "coach" and "referral") and spend time visiting twenty-five coach web sites that closely match what you do or want to do. Write down what you like and do not like about their content and design. Complete the web site content outline. Decide whether you will be designing your site or having someone else design it for you. If you decide to work with a designer, select one whose work you really like.

Coaching Tip: Make your site simple. Make it clear and easy to follow. Make the links, your messages, and your fees easy to find. Don't use huge graphics on your web site. They take forever to load for those who still use older technology to access the Internet. Do not use anything that is too flashy; you run the risk of annoying your visitors.

> **Coaching Tip:** Don't put "Under Construction" anywhere on your web site. All web sites are under construction. I have been working on my web site since 1998. I am always coming up with new programs and fresh ideas. Your web site is a work in progress, because as coaches, we are a work in progress. Don't worry that your web site has to be perfect before it goes live. Develop your web site and get it onto the Internet. You can make updates afterwards.

> **Coaching Tip:** Put your web site on all of your marketing materials and business cards. You want to promote your web site always.

4. Web Automation Tools

There are some tools that can automate your interaction with potential and current clients. These tools can automate the communication, buying, and follow-up process, thus allowing you to concentrate on other things, such as growing your coaching practice. They include:

a. Credit Cards

Estimated Time To Get It Up And Running: 30 Days

Estimated Time To Make Money From It: Immediately

Approximate Cost: $100 To $200 To Set Up. $30-$50 Per Month.

Credit cards automate the payment process and make getting paid simpler. In my experience, 75% of people who do not give you their credit card number at the end of a complimentary call or initial meeting will not make it to their first call. (This statistic is for individual clients only, but you could say that if a potential corporate client does not give you the okay after your first meeting, you will have a long road ahead of you in terms of getting hired.)

Why Take Credit Cards?

1. Buying from you is effortless. Your client does not have to write a check each month, look at the amount, and decide if it is worth it to continue working with you. There is no client time required to take out a stamp

and mail your coaching fee. It may not sound like a lot, but paying you may not be your busy client's top priority.

2. Money is taken out of the equation. There is no chasing checks or money owed to you. As a coach, you want to do what you do best, coach. You don't want to have the "Where is my money?" conversation over and over again.

3. Payments are processed automatically and efficiently.

4. You get paid quickly. Once a credit card payment has been processed, it is deposited into your bank account a few days later. Trips to the bank to deposit checks are unnecessary.

5. You come across professionally. Businesses take credit cards, and you are conveying that you are a business too. Many times a client has said to me, "You do not take credit cards, do you?" When I say yes, they are impressed. I also love to say, "I take credit cards. Which one would you like to use?" and they give me their credit card number. It is a great feeling.

Features You Want:

- A credit card merchant who understands the needs of coaches; that in many cases we do not have a physical location and do most of our work by telephone.

- No hidden charges. Low monthly fees, transaction rates, and costs per usage.

- Free telephone technical support. You also want to be walked though the initial set up at no charge. In addition, you want to get answers to your questions when you have them, not twenty fours hours or later when a representative makes time to reply to your e-mail or voice mail message.

Note: QuickBooks, an excellent accounting program for tracking income and expenses, is another alternative for accepting payments. You can process payments directly within QuickBooks, create paid invoices for your customers, and keep track of your sales and expenses. The credit card software and merchant application is included with your QuickBooks purchase.

b. Shopping Cart Program

Estimated Time To Get It Up And Running: 30 To 60 Days

Estimated Time To Make Money From It: Immediately

Approximate Cost: $25-$75 Per Month

A shopping cart program is a widely accepted system for making purchases on the Internet. It allows you to sell products and services directly from your web site and can accommodate more than one buyer at a time. A shopping cart is just like a retail store, except it is on-line. What you are selling is listed on a web page ready to be purchased.

Why Use A Shopping Cart Program?

- Ease of use and convenience. Buyers shop at their own pace without someone asking them, "Can I help you?" They click on a button, enter their credit card information, and have either purchased your coaching services, one of your e-tools, or a physical product (such as a book or CD) that you have created. The buying process is simple and complete.

- You are giving potential clients access to your products and services 24 hours a day, seven days a week, from anywhere in the world. Your customers are not just visitors in a shopping mall where your store is physically located. They are everywhere.

- The profit is yours. You pay a one-time fee to set up your shopping cart (and a minimal monthly charge) and are ready to go. There are no additional fees, inventory costs, or employees to pay.

- You save money. You do not have to print catalogs, have a special telephone and/or fax number for ordering, and in most cases there are no mailing costs. You incur mailing expenses only if you are selling actual products.

Note: PayPal is also an accepted way to receive money for your coaching programs and products/services. The advantage is you do not have to pay a start-up fee to become a merchant. The disadvantage is the fee per transaction is higher. Either way, you get paid in a few days, and the money is deposited directly into your bank account.

Features You Want:

- A complete system included in one low flat or monthly fee.
- Fast and easy set-up. You want a smooth and error-free ordering process that requires no special technical knowledge to set up or run.
- SSL Encryption for security purposes.
- Fraudulent credit card order protection.
- Transactions authorized in real-time that fully integrate with all payment gateways and methods.
- Transactions processed right on the web, without the need for a separate transaction terminal or processing software.
- A secure, web-based administration area that includes a history of all orders.
- Ability to export names to your mailing lists.
- Ability to send broadcast e-mails and autoresponder messages to people who have bought from you.
- Professionally designed templates to display what you are selling nicely.
- The ability to display a small thumbnail image (a small picture) of the items you are selling.
- The ability to list and sell unlimited items.
- Automatic shipping, gift certificate creation, volume discounts, and tax calculations.
- The creation of customer numbers that stores buying information.
- No 3rd party ads.
- Free telephone technical support with experienced people. (Not outsourced to a different location with only a manual as a main resource to answer your questions.)

c. Broadcast E-Mail

Estimated Time To Get It Up And Running: 30 To 60 Days

Estimated Time To Make Money From It: 60 To 180 Days

Approximate Cost: $25-$75 Per Month

If you are sending out a weekly tip or e-newsletter, automation is the way to go. With a broadcast e-mail mailing list service, all of your e-mail messages go to the same group of people at the same time. This makes the communication process easy and efficient, eliminating the need to send your messages to one person at a time.

An e-mail list is a group of individuals with a common interest. Broadcasting is a one-way method for communicating with these individuals. This is not SPAM or unsolicited email. Only the people who have requested to be on your broadcast e-mail list will get e-mail from you.

Why Use A Broadcast E-Mail Mailing List Service?

- You have access to a targeted group of people who are interested in what you have to say.
- You have easy access to everyone on your list. You can send relevant messages at anytime.
- You save money. E-mailing is cheap. You save paper and postage costs because you are not using regular mail.
- You save time. You will not have to manage e-mail addresses from a lot of different sources such as your regular e-mail address or your address book. They are all in one place.
- You don't need special technical knowledge to spread your message to the world.
- You don't have to manually unsubscribe/subscribe people to your list or handle returned e-mail. This is automatically managed for you.

Features You Want:

- Internet access to your mailing lists at anytime from anywhere in the world. No special software is required.
- Opt-in capability with confirmation that the person who signed up for your e-mail lists has subscribed and their e-mail address is correct. Opt-out capability, to release anyone who doesn't want to continue receiving e-mail from you anymore.
- Automatic handling of returned e-mail, subscribe and unsubscribe requests.
- Import and export features so you can add names and have access to your lists at anytime.
- The HTML code to put on your home page so new subscribers can sign up.
- Personalization of messages. You want to be able to add in a person's first name to your messages if you want to.
- Scheduling capability so you can schedule when e-mail goes out.
- Unlimited number of lists you can create with no additional fees.
- Ability to send e-mail in both text and HTML formats.
- Tracking features to see which web site pages people are clicking to from your e-mail messages.
- No 3rd party ads.
- Password protection for administrative functions.
- Free telephone technical support with experienced people. (Not outsourced to a different location with only a manual as a main resource to answer your questions.)

d. Search Engines

Estimated Time To Get It Up And Running: 30 To 90 Days

Estimated Time To Make Money From It: 90 To 180 Days

Approximate Cost: $30-$2,500 Per Year

The Internet is a key way that potential clients can find and research your coaching programs and services before they decide to contact you. How they find you is either through your promotion or through the use of search engines. When you put in keywords such as "Personal Coach" "Life Coach" or "Career Coach" into a search engine, the search engine searches the entire World Wide Web and returns the names of coaches who fall into this category. Because search engines can sometimes return lists in the hundreds or thousands, if you are at the bottom of the list, you probably will not be found, which leads us to the following:

Why Pay To Get Listed In Search Engines?

Search Engine Optimization companies optimize your web site to get you closer to the top of these lists. They provide a great service because each search engine has its own language and rules on how you can submit your web site for inclusion in their engine. It can be confusing, and therefore, worth it to pay a company to perform this service for you. Because optimization services can be expensive, look for a company that has a proven track record. Ask for sites they have optimized, and do a search on the web to see what type of ranking these companies have.

Features You Want:

- You want a vendor who understands your business and the keywords and META tags that can drive business to your web site.
- An initial and monthly search engine ranking report. You want an analysis of your site and a detailed report that shows where your site ranks today under similar search terms, how you will do tomorrow, and what the actual results are on a monthly basis.
- A vendor who can create META tags for you, which are the keywords search engines use to find you.

- A vendor who will hand submit your site to search engines. Since every search engine has its own rules, hand submissions ensure that you are listed properly.
- You want your site listed within 48 hours or less to top search engines.
- Monthly submissions. You want the work done on a regular basis to ensure that your rankings do not slip.
- Confirmation reports. You want proof stating all submissions were successful.
- Free telephone technical support. You want to get an answer to a question if you have one.

e. Autoresponders

Estimated Time To Get It Up And Running: 30 To 60 Days

Estimated Time To Make Money From It: 60 To 180 Days

Approximate Cost: $18-$75 Per Month

An autoresponder is a software program that automates the process of communicating with potential clients. It automates tedious marketing efforts, reduces hours of administrative work, and increases sales.

The basic premise is potential clients are busy and as a result, may not answer the e-mail you send them the first time you send it. They may even delete it by mistake. An autoresponder increases your chances that a potential client will read your e-mail and respond to it. And because potential clients see your name on a regular basis, they are more likely to remember you when they are ready to hire a coach.

One of the (many) autoresponders on my web site handles complimentary calls. This is how it works. I have blocked out certain times of the week until the end of the year for complimentary calls and I have reserved this time in my calendar. (For example: Mondays between noon and 2 p.m., Tuesdays between 10 a.m. and noon.) When you put in your name and e-mail address into a form on my web site, you get a message that automatically arrives in your inbox. This e-mail gives you a listing of the days and times available for your call. If I do not hear from you in four days, you will get a reminder e-mail to schedule your complimentary call. If I still have not heard from you in 10 days,

25 days, 45 days and 60 days, you will get additional reminder e-mails. You may be wondering why I continue to send e-mail if I have not heard from a potential client. Sometimes things come up and a potential client cannot schedule a call with me at the time they've requested the days and times for their call. Many potential clients thanked me for consistently following up. And when someone does schedule a call, I know they are serious. (Note: when someone schedules a call, I can go into the autoresponder system and easily take them off the list.)

An autoresponder can also be used for paid e-programs or free ones, marketing messages you want to break into smaller pieces, or follow-ups after a sale. See the "Mapping Out Your E-Course" section of this book for how I used an autoresponder to run my 21-Day Career Empowerment Program.

Why Use Autoresponders?

- They are a great lead generator tool. Potential clients do not get lost in e-mail land. This reduces the chance that your e-mail messages will get deleted.
- Messages can consist of free marketing messages or paid e-courses/e-programs.
- Provides a continuous flow of e-mail based on consistent time intervals that you set up.
- Saves time spent disseminating repetitive information. Follows up on information so you do not have to.
- Saves money. E-mail is much easier to use than paper. No paper or postage costs are required.
- Increases the qualification of prospects who contact you. The interested will e-mail or call you after reading one of your autoresponder messages.
- Provides constant marketing with little effort. You set up the stream of messages upfront and the system works effortlessly without your participation.

Features You Want:

- Instant response. You want a prospect to fill out a quick customizable form and get the information they requested into their inbox immediately.
- Opt-in capability with confirmation that the person who signed up for your autoresponder wants to receive it and their e-mail address is correct.
- Unlimited number of follow-up messages.
- Unlimited number of autoresponder lists.
- Unlimited message length.
- Unlimited message changes. You want to be able to make as many changes as you like, 24 hours a day.
- Easy set-up and management. You want to be able to easily cut and paste your messages into the autoresponder system without any special technical knowledge to do so.
- Password protection for administrative functions.
- Import and export features so you can add names and have access to your list at any time.
- Personalization of messages. You want to be able to add a person's first name into your messages if you want to.
- Tracking features to see which autoresponder message are doing the best.
- Automatic handling of returned e-mail, subscribes, and unsubscribes.
- Custom forms as well as the code to put on your web site for people to sign up.
- Ability to send broadcast e-mail to any list.
- No 3rd party ads.
- Blocks unwanted e-mail addresses.
- Free telephone technical support with experienced people. (Not outsourced to a different location with only a manual as a main resource to answer your questions.)

f. Bloggers

Estimated Time To Get It Up And Running: 30 Days

Estimated Time To Make Money From It: 30 To 180 Days

Approximate Cost: None

A blogger is a web-based tool that helps you publish content to the web instantly. A blog is a web page that is part of a blogger that is made up of short, frequently updated messages that are arranged chronologically. The content and purposes of blogs varies greatly, from links and commentary about other web sites, to news about a company/person/idea, to diaries, photos, poetry, mini-essays, project updates, etc. Blog messages are posted to the web instantly.

Why Use A Blogger?

- Bloggers are a cheap way of communicating. You can post messages to the Internet without having to pay a web designer to do this for you.

- Bloggers are instantaneous. You do not have to wait for a web designer's schedule to free up before you can post messages or files on the Internet.

- Bloggers are easy to use. You do not need your own web site or technical knowledge to get started. No software or hardware installation is required.

- Bloggers are interactive. You can easily share thoughts and ideas with clients, potential clients, or other coaches. And they can easily share thoughts and ideas with you.

Features You Want:

Bloggers are very easy to use. You go onto a web site, create a profile, pick a template, and begin. When you want to publish something, you simply enter it into a form. When you're ready, you hit a "Publish" button that automatically sends your message to your blogger. It's very simple and straightforward to use.

Coaching Assignment #8

Make a decision which automation tools you want to use, prioritize their importance to your practice, and plan on when you will implement them. See the Resources section at the back of this book to assist you.

B. Creating An E-Newsletter

Estimated Time To Get It Up And Running: 30 To 60 Days

Estimated Time To Make Money From It: 60 To 180 Days

Approximate Cost: $25-$75 Per Month

One of the most effective methods of bringing traffic to your web site is an e-newsletter. And even though there has been so much written lately about unsolicited e-mail, e-mail that is wanted will be read. E-mail that is sent to those who did not request it will be deleted.

1. Why Write An E-Newsletter?

- E-newsletters are a powerful way to communicate with clients and prospects. You can disseminate information quickly and easily.
- E-newsletters are inexpensive to produce. Your main investment is your time to write them.
- E-newsletters generate leads, increase sales, and position you as an expert.
- The more often potential clients have contact with you, the more comfortable they will be in hiring you as their coach.

The challenge is in creating something that people anticipate, open, read, and pass along to others. Your goal is to make your e-newsletter valuable for the person who is receiving it.

2. Tips For A Successful E-Newsletter

There is so much information today about the dos and don'ts of e-newsletter writing that I've boiled it down to what I consider to be the most important points:

- Put a link to subscribe to your e-newsletter on your web site; your home page is best. Make registration easy; just a few boxes to check and fill out.
- Add links in your e-newsletter to other web sites that are similar to what your target audience wants, but is different from the program(s) you

offer. Cross-marketing with relevant companies and other coaches can bring more traffic to your web site.

- Add links to your web site throughout. Watch out for old or broken links.

- Choose topics that will interest and solve the problems of your target audience. This is how you build loyal readers.

- Write about what you offer. An e-newsletter written about how to be the best parent will only bring you business if you coach parents.

- Make your e-newsletter educational. You can include links and ads in between stories, but if your e-newsletter is only about selling your services, people will unsubscribe.

- Make your e-newsletter opt-in.

- Be real and conversational. Use proper grammar and avoid typos. An e-newsletter that is poorly written sends the wrong impression. A proofreading or editing service will be invaluable if you're not a skilled writer.

- Send out your e-newsletter at least once a month.

- Spread testimonials throughout your e-newsletter. This adds credibility. Endorsements from a third party have more impact than if you said the same words yourself.

- Text is okay. HTML is better. HTML gives your e-newsletter a professional look. It's also more attractive and easier to read. People skip around a lot when they read and the text format is harder to follow.

3. Getting Your E-Newsletter Started

I hear the following from my clients a lot: "What happens if no one likes my writing?" "I am not a very good writer," and "What should I write about?" These are very common questions and reflect a normal response from beginners. I will address each question:

"What happens if no one likes my writing?" Some people will not like your writing. And that's okay. I get e-mail from time to time from people who criticize an article or an e-newsletter issue that I wrote. Feedback is good. It helps me be a better writer. In most cases, my message was not targeted enough, or they were not experiencing what I was writing about. You do not have to get everyone to like you. Focus on touching and inspiring your target audience to take action. If your writing comes from the heart, most people who read it will appreciate what you have written.

"I am not a very good writer." Not everyone is a good writer in the beginning, especially if writing an e-newsletter is new to you. Over time, as you write, you will develop your craft and writing style. When I started writing, I was softer, and now I am more direct. I like who I am as a writer today. Before I was trying to be who I thought my readers wanted me to be. Now I am who I want to be. I get a much better response this way. My husband, who is also the editor for Surpass Your Dreams, edits everything I write. My style and editing skills have grown from his perspective and edits. If you want to be a better writer, take a class, or do what I did, and have someone comment on your work. You can become a good writer if you are committed to it, and let yourself make a few mistakes in the beginning.

"What would I write about?" Many coaches I work with are under the misconception that everything that was supposed to be written has already been written. In a way, this is accurate; there is not a lot of new information. On the other hand, no one has the same perspective as you. No one has gone through what you have gone through in your life or specifically in the same sequence. This is what will make your writing unique; your personal experiences and the message that you want to give to the world.

Coaching Tip: There will always be a reason not to write such as a busy schedule and other things to do in your practice. Writing happens when you sit down and write. It starts out slowly and then the ideas flow. There is a budding writer within you if you want there to be.

---

4. E-Newsletter Template

Here's a template you can use to create an e-newsletter. Even if you do not need every section, this template can help you map out what you want to say and where you want to put it.

Newsletter Name, Date/Year (Put Here)

Welcome to the (Newsletter Name). The goal of this newsletter is to provide you (Put in goal of newsletter here.)

Note: This is an OPT-IN newsletter and ONLY goes to e-subscribers. Unsubscribe information can be found at the end of the e-newsletter.

Your e-mail address will be kept strictly CONFIDENTIAL and will NOT be shared with any other party or mailing list.

##

TABLE OF CONTENTS
I. Article (Can be written by you or someone else.)
II. How To Article (Can be written by you or someone else.)
III.Additional Topic (if any) (Can be written by you or someone else.)
IV. Resources

##

I. ARTICLE

Put Article Here

##

COACHING ADVERTISEMENT (PUT IN SOMETHING YOU WANT THE READER TO BUY)

Put Advertisement Here

##

II. HOW TO ARTICLE

*** Put How To Article Here ***

##

III. ADDITIONAL TOPIC/ADVERTISEMENT/SEMINARS YOU ARE GIVING (if any)

Put Additional Topic/Advertisement/Seminars Here

##

ARE YOU READY FOR (Put your specialty here) COACHING?

(EXAMPLE) Do you wish you had focus? Do you wish you had less to do? Do you wish you could simplify your life? Are you ready to do something about it?

If you answered YES to any of these questions, then coaching may be the next step for you.

Testimonials: (if any)

List Testimonials Here

To schedule your FREE 30-minute telephone coaching call, please send an e-mail to (put e-mail address here) or call (put phone number here).

##

IV. RESOURCES

Put Resources Here

##

GIVE THIS NEWSLETTER TO A FRIEND!

I would appreciate your forwarding this newsletter to your colleagues, friends and family.

To SUBSCRIBE, please visit (put subscribe info here)

To UNSUBSCRIBE, (put unsubscribe info here)

Your e-mail address will be kept strictly CONFIDENTIAL and will NOT be shared with any other party or mailing list.

Have a great month!

(Put your name here) Publisher

Copyright (c) 20__, all rights reserved.

If you do not want to write something this extensive, but want to provide value quickly, consider a weekly action tip. Here's an example of a weekly tip that I wrote:

MONDAY MORNING ACTION TIP #64

REQUEST ASSISTANCE

Look at your messy desk. Your long to-do list. Your overflowing "in-box." Your twenty plus unread email messages, and the stored messages on your voice mail. You are overwhelmed, aren't you? Tasks are piling up, and they are not getting done. Why are you not taking action?

During the daily grind of our careers, we frequently find ourselves drowning in the details. And the daily inertia (the small stuff) holds us back from actively pursuing our career goals. If you are waiting for spare time to take care of the details, you may be waiting for a long time. And while you are waiting, your goals are slipping away.

THE WEEKLY ACTION CHALLENGE

Your challenge this week is to request assistance.

Survey your desk again, but this time, choose one task that has been waiting too long, and then think of people, resources, services, etc. that can assist you in completing that task. Decide precisely what you want done, and then pre-pare a short list of places to turn to for help.

Don't put that list away for tomorrow. Use it now. Make some calls and ask for help. You may get the help you desire or you may not, but at least you will know you gave it your best shot. Asking may not be easy at first. You might be afraid of rejection or hearing the word "no." But the reward of your hard work and effort is locating the person who can help you get things done.

So what do you say? You only have one life to live so it might as well be a life you love.

Have a great week,

Deborah Brown-Volkman (Publisher)
Brian Volkman (Editor)

To SUBSCRIBE, please visit http://www.surpassyourdreams.com and click on the "Monday Morning Action Tips" button to sign up.

To UNSUBSCRIBE, please click on the UNSUBSCRIBE link at the bottom of this e-mail. DO NOT REPLY TO THIS E-MAIL TO UNSUBSCRIBE. If the unsubscribe link does not work, please cut and paste the link into a new browser.

Coaching Assignment #9

Brainstorm topic ideas. Think about what your target audience is interested in. What problems are they having that you can help them solve? List as many ideas as you can.

Coaching Assignment #10

Write your e-newsletter (or your weekly tip). Use the outline and example to get started.

Coaching Tip: To prevent subscribers who forgot that they subscribed to your e-newsletter from crying "You spammed me!" make sure your e-newsletter company provides double opt-in subscriptions. Double opt in assures the spam police that the person who came to your site did request your e-newsletter. Each subscriber gets a confirmation e-mail that asks them to click on a link to confirm their subscription. Yes, this is extra work for your subscribers, and you will lose people who do not click on the confirmation links, but you can be confident that the people on your list want to be there and will hopefully not cause trouble for you in the future. Note: Don't let the threat of the spam police stop you. As long as your e-newsletter has a no spam policy, and you keep track of your subscribers, you are covered.

5. How To Make Money From Your E-Newsletter

As long as you provide valuable content, your subscriber list will grow and subscribers will become loyal readers. Over time they will get to know you very well. My e-newsletter subscribers have seen me through having a full-time job in the corporate world to transitioning into a full-time coaching practice. They wished me well when I got married and at times, they have been my biggest cheerleaders. I put something personal about my life in my e-newsletter when appropriate. My subscribers have responded to this because they got to know something about the person who is behind the words they enjoy.

Because you have a trusted relationship (which you earned and respect), you can advertise your coaching programs and other coaching products/services, and your subscribers will buy them. You can also use your e-newsletter to notify subscribers of upcoming teleclasses, in person workshops, new programs, e-courses, e-books, special times for complimentary calls, etc. Let your subscribers know that they are getting this information first. Exclusivity adds incentive to take you up on your offer(s).

You can also accept advertisements. This is a great way to bring your subscribers' products and services that they will find valuable, while putting money into your bank account at the same time.

The following is the text I have in my e-newsletter that asks people to advertise:

To ADVERTISE, please visit the Surpass Your Dreams Advertising Page for more information. If you want to reach over 13,000 successful senior executives, managers, professionals, and coaches who are looking to enhance their careers and their lives, THIS is an excellent avenue to use!

Here's the copy on my web page that explains the advertising details:

SURPASS YOUR DREAMS NEWSLETTER ADVERTISING INFORMATION
Thank you for your interest in advertising in the "Surpass Your Dreams" e-mail newsletter. If you want to reach over 13,000 successful senior executives, managers, professionals, and coaches who are looking to enhance their careers and their lives, THIS is an excellent avenue to use.

The subscriber breakdown is as follows:

Senior Executives–30% of readership
Managers–35% of readership
Coaches–20% of readership
Professionals–10% of readership
Other (Administrative support, students, etc.)–5% of readership

There are several advertising options:

An ad of up to six lines is $25.00 per issue. Additional lines are $2.00 each. The six lines exclude e-mail addresses and URL's, meaning that you get six lines plus an e-mail address and a URL.

As a SPONSOR, you receive priority placement in the newsletter. You get up to ten lines for $50.00 per issue. Additional lines are $2.50 each. The ten lines exclude e-mail addresses and URL's, meaning that you get ten lines plus an e-mail address and a URL.

Ad Guidelines:

- We reserve the right to reject any ad we find objectionable for whatever reason.
- All lines are a maximum of 70 characters including spaces, periods, commas, etc.
- All ads must be prepaid.
- No refunds are issued once the newsletter has been finalized.
- You agree to indemnify, defend, and save harmless Deborah Brown-Volkman and Surpass Your Dreams from any and all liabilities, including attorney fees, resulting from the claims you make in your advertisements.

C. Writing Articles

Estimated Time To Get It Up And Running: 30 To 60 Days

Estimated Time To Make Money From It: 60 To 360 Days

Approximate Cost: $25-$75 Per Month

Articles are an excellent tool for showcasing your knowledge and expertise. When an article is published, it means that a third party likes it and says it has merit. (I like when someone calls me or sends me an e-mail saying that they saw my article in a publication. It makes me feel like the effort I put into writing articles is worthwhile.) Well written articles that are packed with useful information can bring potential clients into your coaching practice.

Articles are also a great way to get free advertising. I get many requests from sales people who want me to advertise in their newspapers and magazines at a very high cost. I tell them that I advertise by providing content. Many of them take me up on this offer because good content is very valuable and hard to come by.

1. Why Write Articles?

- Articles are a great way to communicate with potential clients. You can disseminate information quickly and easily.
- Articles can help you spread your message and opinions to many people.
- Articles are inexpensive to produce. Your main investment is the time it takes to write them.
- Articles position you as an expert and generate leads.
- The more often potential clients see your writing, the more comfortable they will feel about hiring you.

2. Tips For Articles That Get Read And Have Great Impact

- Write articles about topics that will interest your target audience and solve their problems.
- Be real. Let the reader know that you understand what they are going through, and that your article is going to help them with their specific difficulty.

- Write about what you know and can offer. An article written about how to speak effectively in front of an audience will only bring you clients if you are a public speaking coach.

- Articles should be "how-to" in nature and have between 500 to 750 words per article. Make them easy to read and packed with useful content.

- Articles should be no more than 65 characters per line. Anything more than that and you get jaggedly lines when you send them out by e-mail.

- Finish your article before you distribute it. Eliminate typos and spelling errors. Many times I receive article submissions for my Surpass Your Dreams e-newsletter and I reject them because they would take too much time and energy to get them ready for publication. Find people to proofread your article before it goes out.

- Do not send your articles as attachments. Cut and paste them into an e-mail.

- Do not get discouraged if you do not get feedback right away. You are building a relationship over time. Readers and editors want to know that you are not a one-time fluke. Articles distributed on a regular basis (approximately once a month) will bring results.

- Read a lot. Magazines, newspapers, and e-newsletters are a great source for generating new ideas. Reading can be the catalyst for writing what has not been said or for providing a different perspective on a current idea.

- Keep writing. Writing gets easier over time. The first article can be the hardest to write because the possibility of rejection is scary. The positive comments you receive from readers whose lives you have touched can be enough to eliminate your initial concerns.

3. How To Write An Article

Start with a problem your target audience is experiencing. Consider how your article can offer a solution, or be an introduction to a solution.

Brainstorm some ideas, then create an outline. This will help you stay focused and on track. Create a catchy title. This will grab the reader's interest. The first paragraph should ask questions with which the reader can associate with. Fill in the rest of the article with valuable, how-to information. End with a call to action or a conclusion as well as a byline that is a sort of classified ad. Make this a compelling invitation to visit your web site or call you. Add a cover letter that explains who you are and why you think your article is a fit for the editor's publication. Once you have these elements in place, you are ready to go.

4. Article And Cover Letter Sample

Here's an example of a cover letter and article that I wrote. This article was picked up and an expanded version was published by the *Wall Street Journal*.

Subject: New Article—Career Distress? Being Inspired Is Your Answer.

Hello,

Here is a new article for your consideration. I am hoping that you will find the unique information from **"Career Distress? Being Inspired Is Your Answer"** extremely useful.

Please feel free to publish the article below along with my Resource box or include it in one of your stories. I would appreciate a courtesy copy when it goes out.

Allow me a quick introduction. My name is Deborah Brown and I am the president of Surpass Your Dreams, a successful career and mentor coaching company, based in Long Island, NY.

We work with senior executives, vice presidents, and managers who are out of work or overworked.

I am also the president of the United Coaching Associates, a Long Island based organization that provides ongoing training and development for coaches, as well as being a resource for those who are looking for the perfect business or personal coach.

I have been quoted as a career expert by the *Wall Street Journal*, the *New York Times*, *Smart Money Magazine*, and *New York Newsday*, as well as having been interviewed by *Entrepreneur Magazine* and *Business 2.0*.

More info can be found at my Media Relations page at:

http://www.surpassyourdreams.com/media.html

My telephone number and e-mail information are below. Please feel free to contact me at anytime.

Thank you for the opportunity to contribute to your purpose and mission.

Deborah

****

Deborah Brown-Volkman, Career & Mentor Coaching
President, Surpass Your Dreams
http://www.surpassyourdreams.com
President, United Coaching Associates
http://www.unitedcoachingassociates.com
info@surpassyourdreams.com

ARTICLE: CAREER DISTRESS? BEING INSPIRED IS YOUR ANSWER

Many people I speak with are looking for that magic formula, the recipe that will transform their careers. The truth is they may never find what they are looking for. The reason is they are looking outward, when the answer is within.

I've seen many individuals create amazing careers. Even in a tough job market when they are told there are no jobs, they are still securing positions that they love. How are they doing it? They are inspired.

Inspiration is that almighty force that arises from the inside. It lights you up and gives you more power than you ever expected. Think about a time in your career when you were excited and energized because everything was going your way. Can you imagine being able to apply that feeling to where you are today?

<u>What Will You Do Differently If You Are Inspired?</u>

1. You Will Call The Person You've Been Afraid To Call

You will find yourself picking up the telephone and having conversations with people that get them excited. You will be able to articulate exactly what you want, and be amazed as the person on the other end extends a hand to help you.

2. You Will Send The E-Mail You've Been Afraid Of Sending

You will stop telling yourself that people are too overwhelmed to read your e-mail. You will write e-mails that inspire people to take action, and they will. Your creativity will be at its height, and your words will flow easily.

3. You Will Send The Letters You've Been Afraid To Send

You will find yourself buying the finest paper so your words can stand out. You will find the addresses of the people you want to contact effortlessly. The people to whom you write will read your letters because they will want to know more about the passionate person who wrote them.

4. You Will Meet The People You've Been Afraid To Meet

You will get out and network with the people you have been staying away from. You will find yourself describing what you want eloquently, and the people you speak with will understand you and refer you to someone who can assist you. You will enjoy yourself and be comfortable in the surroundings of people you do not know. People will want to know who you are, and your magnetism will be the catalyst that creates the relationship.

5. You Will Have The Conversations You've Been Afraid To Have

You will speak to the people in your life and ask for the support you need to move forward. You will apologize and take responsibility for expecting them to read your mind. You will acknowledge them for the gift they have been in your life. You will tell them what you want and why it is important that you receive it from them. They will appreciate your honesty and provide you with the assistance you need.

6. You Will Conquer Your Fears

And your life will never be the same.

So, how do you get inspired? You put your disappointments behind you because you realize how much they are holding you back. You recognize that your career gets better when you make it better. You write down your vision on a piece of paper, and you look at it every day. Then you put a plan in place to get it.

A great career does not only happen to other people. It can happen to you.

So what do you say? You only have one life to live so it might as well be a life you love!

Add A Signature Tag:

**Deborah Brown-Volkman is the president of Surpass Your Dreams, a career and mentor coaching company that has been delivering a message of motivation, success, and personal fulfillment since 1998. We work with senior executives, vice presidents, and managers, who are out of work or overworked, and coaches who want to build profitable coaching practices.

Deborah is also the president of the United Coaching Associates, a Long Island based organization that provides ongoing training and development for coaches, as well as being a resource for those who are looking for the perfect business or personal coach.

To learn more visit: http://www.surpassyourdreams.com or send an e-mail to info@surpassyourdreams.com.

NOTE: I DO NOT INTEND TO SPAM ANYONE. I only send articles to those who are interested in hearing from me. If you would prefer not to receive articles from me in the future, please click on the UNSUBSCRIBE link at the end of this e-mail. (Note: I put this at the bottom of every article I send out.)

Coaching Assignment #11

Write an article and cover letter. Create a signature tag at the end that describes what you do. Use my example to help you get started.

5. How To Get Your Articles Published

Once you have written your article, it's time to get it published. There are several ways to do this:

1) Submit your article to article directories. These directories were created for editors and e-zine publishers who need free content for their on-line or printed publications. The directories are listed by subject and are categorized for easy access. Editors fill out a form that states that they understand that your work is yours and cannot be used unless your contact information is at the bottom of the article. Once they agree, your article has the potential to reach thousands of readers. To find a list of article directories, go to the web, and do a search under the keywords "Article Directories." You will find many web sites to choose from.

2) Build your own database of editors. Identify magazines, newspapers, and on-line publications that relate to your field of expertise. I did a search on the Internet, and looked for career sites, job boards, search firms, and other sites related to getting a new job or being more effective in the one you have. I collected the e-mail addresses of the people who were in charge of marketing. These are the people who want their web site to be the best it can be. I also went to Yahoo.com and did a search under newspapers and magazines. Since I am a career coach, I looked for editors who were responsible for producing career related articles.

Search for editors who are responsible for the area you are writing about. If your articles are not relevant to them, they will not read it. If editors are not identified by area, send your article and cover letter to the most senior editor on the team.

Utilizing both strategies can be very effective. To date, my articles have been published in over 100 web sites and printed publications. The growth of my e-newsletter mailing list and the success of my e-products can be attributed directly to people reading my articles and then visiting my site to find out more. Start small and grow your list one name at a time. One day you will be impressed by the number of e-mail addresses you have in your database.

D. Electronic Books (E-Books)

Estimated Time To Get It Up And Running: 90 To 180 Days

Estimated Time To Make Money From It: 180 To 270 Days

Approximate Cost: $30 To $750 To Create

An e-book is a book that is not converted to paper format. You write it on-line (usually in a word processing software program) and you sell and distribute it on-line. There is no page limit. An e-book can be as short as ten pages or as long as you want.

E-books are a great way to bring in passive revenue. Passive revenue is money that you make as a result of effort you put into something just once (creating the e-book) and that brings in the reward (money) over and over again. You write your e-book, put it on your web site, and sell it. That's it. You do not have to be working all the time to make money.

1. Why Write An E-Book?

- People want information fast. An e-book fulfills this need. No waiting for information because it is delivered automatically. You provide instant gratification.
- More and more people are getting access to the web each day. You can sell your e-book to the world, 24 hours a day, seven days a week. You can reach many more people than if you developed a paper book and sold it locally.
- You are able to provide information in a timely fashion. Paper books can take up to a year to create. The information you want to distribute may be outdated by then.
- Convenience. You have knowledge and experience on a particular topic. There are people who want to know what you know, and they will pay you for it.
- You don't have to deal with publishers or other people who have to approve your work before it can be published. You also can edit your e-book at any time.
- There are no printing, shipping, or postage costs.

- No other work is required once the initial work is done. You are able to use your time to create other projects or get additional coaching clients.

- Those who may not be able to afford your one-on-one coaching fee or want to try you out first before hiring you will be able to do so.

My first e-book, "Living A Life You Love. The Pathway To Personal Freedom," was easy to create. I took eleven of my most popular career articles, arranged them in sequential order that made sense to the reader, and added worksheets at the end of each article with four to six questions for the reader to complete. A workbook of sorts. I began by charging $14.95 and later lowered the price to get more orders. I have sold a lot of e-books. Not bad for a one time amount of work.

Coaching Tip: There are many coaches who create e-books and give them away for free. I do not believe you should do this. It takes time and energy to create an e-book. If you want to give information away, use your e-newsletter or articles instead. Just because an e-book is not in paper format does not mean it does not have the same value as a paper-based book. Your words have meaning and value and should be sold for a price that compensates you for your time.

---

2. How To Write An E-Book

- Brainstorm some topics that are relevant to your target audience. Pick a problem they are experiencing, and make your e-book their solution.

- Get feedback on your ideas. Ask a few people what they think. If you get, "Wow, that is a great idea!" you are on track. If people look at you strangely, it may mean you have the wrong title or topic. Make sure the people you ask are part of your target audience.

- Select a topic. "How-To" titles sell the best.

- Map out your e-book; what you will be covering and in what order.

- Write. Do not worry if your grammar is not perfect. Get your ideas out. Write the best content that you can. You will edit your work later.

- Write a few pages at a time. You do not want to overwhelm yourself with having to do too much at once. You also do not want to rush the process.

A few written pages every day or every other day will give you a completed first draft shortly.

- Take time away from your e-book. The perspective will be good for you and your e-book.
- Edit your work.
- Ask two people you trust to read and edit your e-book. Give them a time frame so the project does not drag out.
- Edit your e-book.
- Edit it again.
- Edit it again. (No, this is not a misprint. You want to produce the best work you can, which means editing your e-book a few times before it is complete.)
- Finish your e-book. Add the finishing touches such as disclaimers, copyright information, your bio, resources, etc.
- Create a catchy title. Example: the seven steps to…change your life in seven days.
- Decide how much you will charge. (Note: This may change over time. In the beginning, you will be testing the marketplace to see how it sells. You could raise or lower the price based on demand or other factors. In addition, look at others in your area of expertise to see if they have an e-book and what they are charging.)
- Find someone (or do it yourself) to convert your e-book into PDF, HTML, EXE or another e-book compatible format so it can be downloaded from your web site. (Note: PDF or Portable Document Format means your e-book is being created with Adobe Acrobat. EXE or an executable file means your e-book is being created with an e-book compiler. HTML or Hyper Text Markup Language means your e-book is being created to be read directly from your web site. PDF is considered to be the industry standard for e-book publishing.) Make sure your e-book is easy to read, loads quickly, has no spelling errors, and that all of the links work well.
- Find someone (or do it yourself) who can create a cover for you as well as provide the JPEG graphic you can put in your web site.
- Find someone (or do it yourself) to add your e-book to your on-line shopping cart program and your web site.

3. Mapping Out Your E-Book

Mapping out the content is important because this sets the foundation for your e-book. Think logically. Put yourself in the shoes of the reader. What sequence would you want to walk through to get the desired result your e-book is promising? Once you have this sequence clear in your mind, take your topic, and break it into smaller pieces. List the pieces in sequential order. This will become your table of contents. Once you have the table of contents completed, fill in the chapters.

Here's my outline, which turned into my table of contents. "Living A Life You Love. The Pathway To Personal Freedom" was designed to help the reader discover their ideal career by discovering themselves first.

> **Coaching Tip:** You can use the same thought process to create a book. The main difference is instead of putting your words into an e-format, you will be putting your words on paper.

4. A Sample Chapter

CHAPTER NINE–COACH YOUR CRITIC OUT!

The infamous inner critic, you know, that little voice inside your head that says you can't, until you're pretty darn sure it's right. Well, it's not. It's dead wrong, I'm going to give you the surefire cure to oust your critic now.

1. Tactic One: Know Your Enemy.

In order to fight the good fight, you have to recognize the enemy. In other words, you must spend some time getting to know your own thinking process. Take a day to listen from the inside out instead of the outside in. What are you saying to yourself? When a great idea pops into your head what do you do with it? Many people diminish it until the good idea is but a mere memory. So listen close and hear what your personal inner critic sounds like.

2. Tactic Two: Talk Back

Isn't it interesting that we won't accept someone else putting us down, but we are quite content to let our inner critic do us in? Quit being your own worst enemy. When you hear "I can't," talk back immediately. You can talk your inner critic back into silence. It's not fond of fighting.

3. Tactic Three: Write It Down To Size

Yes indeed, the pen is a powerful tool. Once you have learned to recognize the inner critic, and you've started talking back, keep it in its place by writing it out. This takes a little more time and a little more discipline but in the long run you will come out ahead. Write down all the finicky, frustrating thoughts in your head. Write freely with no editing, no reading, and no rereading. Just get it out. Vent and complain, about everything on your mind. Then you'll be rid of the clutter that can keep you from succeeding. But you are not finished. Write out your affirmations. All those great things that you want to do, be, and achieve. Write them like they have already happened. Believe it or not, it will start to sink into your subconscious until you find yourself making these things happen.

4. Tactic Four: Be Nice to Yourself

This is permission to be a little crazy. In fact, this exercise might make you feel a little funny at first, but if you keep at it, in time you won't even be able to find your inner critic. Nothing makes it shrink like a face-to-face showdown. So gather your courage and look in the mirror. Instead of criticizing yourself, as we so often do, give yourself some encouragement. Biblically we are told to treat our neighbors like ourselves. If we did that, our neighbors would move. (Unless we start treating ourselves better.) Write down five great things about yourself and read them everyday. Before long, you'll begin to see that you are right. You have amazing potential and superb ideas. You are on the verge of making your goals a reality.

WORKSHEET #9

Now, let's start by turning these tactics into actions:

List five critical things you say to yourself:

1.
2.
3.
4.
5.

List five positive things you could say to yourself instead:

1.
2.
3.
4.
5.

Over the next seven days, make a check for every day you wrote your frustrations in your journal.

1.
2.
3.
4.
5.
6.
7.

List how you will reward yourself for doing this for one full week.

1.
2.
3.
4.
5.

Can you see that you are on the right road? By changing how you think, you also change how you act or react to any given situation. You have the inner power to feel completely different about yourself. In turn, this will make tremendous things happen for you.

Coaching Assignment #12

Create an outline for your e-book and begin to fill in the chapters.

5. How To Promote Your E-Book

The promotion of your e-book is up to you. Create a separate page for your e-book on your web site and list this page in search engines. List your e-book in e-book directories and announcement forums. Give your e-book to a few people and ask them to spread the word. Send a press release to the media. Offer a discount to your e-newsletter subscribers. Tell everyone you know.

E. Electronic Courses (E-Courses)

Estimated Time To Get It Up And Running: 30 To 90 Days

Estimated Time To Make Money From It: 90 To 180 Days

Approximate Cost: $18-$75 Per Month

E-courses are another great way to brining passive revenue into your coaching practice. An e-course is a series of related lessons that are distributed at regular intervals via an automated email service known as an autoresponder. You create the e-course upfront, you get paid upfront, and the lessons come automatically to the people who ordered your e-course for as many days as the e-course lasts. Your participation is not required.

1. Why Write An E-Course?

- An e-course can be created easily and quickly. No technical knowledge is necessary.
- You make money 24 hours a day, seven days a week.
- E-courses are completely automated. Unlike an e-newsletter that goes out on a schedule that you determine, an e-course starts at the moment someone requests it.
- E-courses are self-directed. Lessons come right to their in-box. No additional input is required from you.
- The purchaser learns on their own. There are no schedule conflicts between you and the person who buys your e-course.
- You can take your time to teach something. There are no word constraints that are common with an article or e-newsletter. An e-course can be as short or long as you want.
- No other work is required once the initial work is done. You are able to use your time to create other projects or work with clients.

> **Coaching Tip:** Because e-courses are delivered by e-mail, you are at the mercy of the World Wide Web. On some days, because of a peculiarity of a user's e-mail system, a lesson may not be delivered. This is common and the main drawback of e-courses. To get around this problem, create a page on your web site where users can download your entire e-course. So, if they don't receive a lesson, they can go to this web page to retrieve it. This is the message I have put on my web site to address this problem:

2. How To Write An E-Course

The process is very similar to creating an e-book.

- Brainstorm a few topics that are relevant to your target audience. Pick a problem that they are experiencing and make your e-course their solution.
- Get feedback on your ideas. Ask a few people what they think. If you get "Wow, that is a great idea!" you are on track. If people look at you strangely, it may mean you have a title or topic that is not resonating with people at the moment. Make sure the people you ask are a part of your target audience.
- Select a topic. "How-To" titles sell best.
- Map out your e-course; what you will be covering and in what order.
- Write. Do not worry if the grammar is perfect or not. Get your ideas out. Write a few days at a time. Focus on writing the best content that you can. You will edit your work later.
- Take time away from your e-course. The perspective will make your e-course stronger.
- Edit your work.
- Edit your e-course.
- Edit it again.
- Edit it again. (yes, again.)
- Ask two people to read and take your e-course. Request that they take the course every day if possible. Ask for specific thoughts and recommendations based on what worked and did not work. Give them

a time frame so the project does not drag out. Tweak what needs to be tweaked. Leave alone what is effective.

- Edit and complete your e-course.
- Create a catchy title. Example: the seven steps to…change your life in seven days.
- Finish your e-course.
- Decide how much you will charge. Pick a price and see how your e-course sells. (You can always tweak it later.) In addition, look at others in your area of expertise to see if they have an e-course and what they are charging.
- Research and select an autoresponder company and enter your lessons onto their web site. (Note: There are recommendations for autoresponder companies at the end of this book.)
- Find someone (or do it yourself) who can create a logo for your e-course. You want a JPEG graphic you can put onto your web site.
- Find someone (or do it yourself) to add your e-course to your on-line shopping cart program and your web site.

Coaching Tip: To charge or not to charge? It depends. I am a big believer in getting paid for your time and effort. Other coaches will tell you they want to grow their practices so they will give away whatever they can. If you have valuable information that is not found easily in other places, charge for your e-course. However, if you wrote an article and want to break it into smaller pieces so people can get a taste of your coaching style, give your e-course away for free.

---

3. Mapping Out Your E-Course

Map out the content for your e-course before you begin to write it. Put yourself in the shoes of the person who is taking your e-course. What sequence would you want to walk through to get the desired result your e-course is promising? List all the steps, and then put them into sequential order.

Here's the outline for my 21-Day Career Empowerment Program that was the foundation for my e-course. This e-course was designed for senior executives, vice presidents, and managers who are contemplating a career change, but want to be sure before they make their move. Once I completed this e-course, I created a version for college students who want direction in their career now rather than later in life.

Autoresponder Messages for 21-Day Career Empowerment Program

Subject	Day
Welcome to the 21-Day Career Empowerment Program!	0
Day #1: Am I In The Right Career?	1
Day #2: What Do I Like To Do?	2
Day #3: What Do I Dislike To Do?	3
Day #4: What Have I Always Wanted To Do?	4
Day #5: What Are My Strengths & Weaknesses?	5
Day #6: Where Do I Want To Be Located?	6
Day #7: What Industry Do I Want To Work In?	7
Day #8: What Kind Of Structure Do I Need?	8
Day #9: How Many Hours Do I Want To Spend Working?	9
Day #10: Do I Want To Work In An Office Or From My Home?	10
Day #11: Do I Want To Work Inside Or Outside?	11
Day #12: How Much Do I Want To Earn?	12
Day #13: What Type Of People Do I Want To Work With?	13
Day #14: Do I Want To Work In A Fast Or Slow Paced Atmosphere?	14
Day #15: Am I Using My Skills And Talents?	15
Day #16: Do I Want To Work For Someone Else Or Myself?	16
Day #17: Do I Want To Lead Or Follow?	17
Day #18: Do I Want To Work By Myself Or With A Team?	18
Day #19: Do I Want To Be A Specialist Or A Generalist?	19
Day #20: Do I Want To Keep My Current Career Long-Term?	20
Day #21: Am I In The Right Career?	21

I chose to make my program 21 days because I've heard that it takes 21 days to form a new habit and I wanted to capitalize on this well-known number. The questions are very simple and straightforward. I tell my clients that they could probably run through all 21 questions in one hour, but not to do so. The e-course was created so they can think about one question every day. Before they bought the e-course, my clients have not taken the time to think about their careers and this is a major reason why they are dissatisfied. This is why I want them to take their time.

4. A Sample Lesson

DAY #12: HOW MUCH DO I WANT TO EARN?

Lots of money, of course! But realistically, it is much better to have a specific number in your head so you know what to aim at. What do you need money for? A better home, car, vacation, clothes, early retirement? How much do you need to pay your bills? Add up your monthly expenses and multiply that number by 12. Include what you want in your savings account each year, as well as the amount you want for future purchases. What figure did you arrive at? This is what your career should be paying you. Now it is time to make it happen!

Before I became a coach, I ran trade shows and events programs for Fortune 500 companies and dot-coms. Everyone familiar with the field said that event planners were not paid well. Meanwhile, I was getting paid more and more as I progressed in my career. How did I do it? I asked for what I wanted. And if they said what I was asking for was not in the budget, I showed them the value they would receive from hiring me. I would bring in pictures from past trade shows and events and show them what was possible. During interviews, potential employers not only saw my skills, they saw my passion. I always got paid what I requested.

TODAY'S QUESTION

How much do you want to get paid? Write down your answer. Start making room in your life for more money!

Coaching Assignment #13

Create an outline for your e-course and fill in the days.

5. How To Promote Your E-Course

Just like the marketing of an e-book, the promotion of your e-course is up to you. Create a separate page for your e-course on your web site and list this page in search engines. Have a few people take your e-course for free in exchange for testimonials. Ask them to spread the word. Send a press release to the media. Offer a discount to your e-newsletter subscribers. Tell everyone you know.

3-2: Speaking As A Marketing Strategy

Speaking is effective and it works. When you speak, you are giving potential clients immediate access to you, your opinions, and the program(s) you have created to solve their problems. Speaking can bring new clients into your coaching practice.

I break speaking into two marketing strategy pieces: in person and by telephone. For example, you can speak in person at a local chamber of commerce or networking event, or over the telephone when you lead a teleclass. Here's how to utilize speaking as an effective marketing strategy to become a profitable coach.

A. Speaking: Live And In Person

Estimated Time To Get It Up And Running: 60 To 180 Days

Estimated Time To Make Money From It: 180 To 360 Days

Approximate Cost: $0 To $5,000 to get it up and running. (Cost can include the books and coaching to get ready, photocopies that need to be made before each presentation, and the items you create to sell in the back of the room.)

For years, I was convinced that I could create a profitable practice through writing alone. Believe me, I gave it my best shot. I built a pretty comprehensive web site with all the bells and whistles. I got numerous clients this way. (I still do.) But still, many potential clients want to see you before they hire you.

I never thought speaking could make that much of an impact until I took myself out of my office and hit the road. Then, I saw the results for myself. I started giving presentations about how to excel in your career with a fellow coach, Andrea Feinberg, who can be found at www.coachinginsight.com. Teaming up with her was the catalyst that got me out the door.

I also worked with a presentation skills coach (Great investment!) Rachel Spaulding, my coach, transformed the way I appear in front of an audience. Rachel can be found at: www.live-it-coach.com

1. Why Speak In Front Of A Live Audience?

- You gain immediate access to potential clients.
- You gain immediate access to people who can refer you to potential clients.
- You build credibility face-to-face.
- You get known for being an expert.
- You are able to reach many people at one time.
- You get to speak to people who want to hear what you have to say as they have taken time from their busy day to come see you (This is a great confidence booster!).
- You have the opportunity to see if what you are saying makes sense. Audiences don't lie. If they like what you are saying, you will know it immediately; you will see their reactions. If they do not get your message or your presentation style, then you have the opportunity to learn from the experience, and you can strengthen your message and improve your presentation for the next time.

2. Tips To Ensure That Your Presentation Goes Well

Even the most experienced speaker has things to worry about. You may worry whether you will find the location and arrive on time. You may worry about how you look, and whether the audience will like what you are wearing. You may worry about having all of your materials photocopied on time, and whether the audience will keep them or throw them away. Here are some tips to increase the odds of shining on the day of your presentation.

- Send your requirements to the person who is running the meeting beforehand. Get there early and check everything before you go on. This way there are no surprises, and even if there are some (you can't control everything), you will have time to fix them.
- Be educational. Do not sell during your presentation. The audience is there to learn, not to be sold to. If they learn something new and like the way you presented the material, they may become new clients. If you try to sell them, you will watch the back of their heads as they walk out the door.
- Speak about your target audience's problems and provide solutions during your presentation. Be empathetic. Use client examples and success

stories. (Do not use real names!) Build rapport with the audience. You want them to know that you understand what they are going through, that either you or your clients have gone through the same thing, and that you know exactly what it takes to get to the other side.

- Use handouts. I find they are most effective when used during the presentation rather than giving them out afterwards. You can ask the audience to follow what you are saying, and in most instances, it makes what you are saying clear. Plus, if you are nervous, it takes the focus off you at certain times during your presentation.

- Ask for a written evaluation at the end; you want to keep what works and eliminate what does not work for future presentations.

- Stick around after your presentation is over. Members of the audience will want to talk with you, especially if you did a good job. Some people will say, "Thank you," and others will give you their business cards because they want to speak with you about their current situation.

- Bring products to sell at the back of the room. In many cases, you do not get paid to speak, so you want to be able to make money in other ways.

Coaching Tip: Practice, practice, and practice again before you give your presentation. You can never over prepare. The more you practice, the less nervous you will feel when it is time to go on.

Coaching Tip: When you are presenting, speak passionately. Even a boring topic can be interesting if you sound excited while saying it. Give it your all; do not hold back. Enjoy the moment and give a presentation that makes you proud.

---

3. Places To Get A Live Speaking Gig

There are many different places to speak. They include:

- Associations
- Bookstores
- Business Groups

- Chambers Of Commerce
- Colleges And Universities
- Economic Development Agencies
- Kiwanis Clubs
- Libraries
- Hospitals
- Networking Organizations
- Rotary Clubs
- Venture Groups
- Women's Groups

Most groups have monthly meetings for which they need speakers. Your goal is not to speak "everywhere" but in front of your target audience.

Coaching Assignment #14

Open the phone book or search on the Internet to locate organizations or groups that are in your area. Find out if they need speakers (either this year or next) and the type of people who are members and/or attend their meetings or events. If it's a match, get the contact information for the person who books speakers.

4. Speaking Outline Sample

A speaking outline is important because it details what you will be talking about. It gives the person who books speakers time to evaluate whether your topic would be a fit for their group. Make sure your headline is catchy and your outline addresses and solves a problem your target audience is experiencing. You don't want to speak in front of a group that is not interested in the solution your presentation will be providing. Note: Yes, you never know who will be in the room, but since your time is valuable, it makes sense to speak in front of as many people as possible who can actually hire you.

Here is a copy of an outline and bio I use:

JUMP START YOUR CAREER WITH INSPIRATION. FIVE WAYS TO GET UNSTUCK AND MOVING AGAIN.

Many people I speak with are looking for that magic formula, the recipe that will transform their careers. The truth is they may never find what they are looking for. Why? Because they are looking outward, when the answer is within.

I've helped hundreds of individuals create amazing careers. Even in this job market, when they are told there are no jobs, or resources are low, they are still creating careers they love. How are they doing it? They are inspired.

In a recent CEO/Top Executive Survey, passion for what done does was cited as the second most important career motivator. Why is this so vital for you to know? Because you cannot find a career that you are passionate about, or rediscover the passion you once had for your present career, without being inspired first.

IN THIS LIVELY AND INTERACTIVE PRESENTATION, YOU WILL LEARN:

- Why inspiration is the secret to having a career you love
- Why getting inspired again is easier that you think
- How to jump start your career and get back into action quickly
- How to use inspiration to create a career plan that will work
- How to tap into the power of inspiration for yourself so you can transform your career and your life

MY BIO: (Your bio showcases your background and credentials to speak about the topic.)

Deborah Brown-Volkman is the president and founder of Surpass Your Dreams, Inc., a career and mentor coaching that has been delivering a message of motivation, success, and personal fulfillment since 1998. Deborah is also the president and founder of the United Coaching Associates, a Long Island based organization that provides ongoing training and development for coaches, as well as being a resource for those who are looking for the perfect business or personal coach. For her career coaching clients, Deborah works with senior executives, vice presidents, and managers who are out of work and over-worked. For her mentor coaching clients, Deborah works with coaches who want to start and build profitable coaching practices.

Deborah is a published writer and motivational speaker. She has been quoted in *the Wall Street Journal,* the *New York Times, Smart Money Magazine,* the *Chicago Tribune,* and *New York Newsday,* and has been interviewed by *Entrepreneur Magazine* and *Business 2.0.* She was also a featured guest on BBC, Radio Scotland when they came to New York City to find out how people were coping in their careers since the September 11th attacks.

Deborah has worked with individuals from companies such as JPMorgan Chase, Oracle Corporation, Lucent Technologies, General Motors, Procter & Gamble, Ziff Davis, American Express, EDS, Ogilvy & Mather, McCann-Erickson Worldgroup, Columbia University, New York University, Chief Executive Magazine, MSNBC, and BMW.

Before Deborah became a full-time coach, her background included twelve years managing sales and marketing programs for Fortune 500 companies and dot-coms. She received an A.A.S. degree in data processing from Queensborough Community College, a B.A. in marketing from Hofstra University, and a certificate in financial planning from New York University. Deborah is a graduate of Coach U, and is pursuing her advanced coach training through CoachVille's Graduate School of Coaching,

Deborah and her husband Brian live in Long Island, NY.

Coaching Assignment #15

Part I. Create a speaking outline and bio. Make sure that each one is no longer than one page.

Part II. Identify 10 places to send your speaking outline and bio. Distribute them by e-mail or regular mail. Then, use the telephone to follow up. Follow-up is key to getting speaking invitations.

5. Speaker's Evaluation Form

An evaluation form is an effective way to get feedback and a confidential method for following up with people who may be interested in working with you after your presentation. (Note: if the situation does not allow the opportunity to hand out an evaluation form, ask the people who are interested in having you contact them hand you their business card before they leave.)

Here's an example of an evaluation form I use:

Thank you for joining me this evening. I hope you found the presentation to be stimulating, fun and informative. I enjoyed being with all of you! Please take a few moments to answer the questions below. Your comments and suggestions make a difference. I will incorporate them into future presentations.

1. Did the description of the presentation match what you heard?

Yes ___
No ___

2. Was the presentation clear?

Yes ___
No ___

If no, why not?

_____

_____

3. Did you learn something new from the presentation?

Yes ___
No ___

If yes, what did you learn?

_____

_____

4. Do you have comments or suggestions on how to improve this presentation?

If yes, please provide them:

_____

_____

5. Would you recommend this presentation to someone else?

Yes ___
No ___

If yes, who? (Please provide their name, organization name, e-mail address, and telephone number.)

_____

_____

_____

_____

6. May I add you to my e-newsletter mailing list?

Yes ___
No ___

If yes, what is your e-mail address?

_____

7. Are you interested in one-on-one coaching?

Yes ___
No ___

Optional information:

Your name: _____

Your e-mail address: _____

Your telephone number: _____

If you would like to contact me, I can be reached by e-mail at (add your e-mail address), by telephone at: (add your phone number), or via web at: (add your web site address)

Thank you again for coming.

6. Turning Attendees Into Paying Clients

You are speaking to meet potential clients. Make it easy for them to reach you after your presentation. Provide handouts with your contact information on the bottom. Give away coaching as a raffle prize, and obtain the business cards of the people who drop them into the bowl. (Set up a bowl first.) Before your presentation, schedule open times in your calendar for complimentary calls and/or initial meetings, and schedule these on the spot.

Follow up, follow up and follow up. I cannot stress this enough. You want to speak with people while your presentation is still fresh in their minds. By not following up immediately, you are throwing away potential business. Call or e-mail people the day after your presentation; tell them about a special offer you are making to the people who attended. Thank them again for being there.

7. Getting Paid As A Speaker

There will come a point when, instead of inviting yourself to speak, invitations will come to you. This means that you are in demand and can request payment for your time. Groups, chambers of commerce, and associations do offer honorariums for speakers they want at their meetings or events. When asked what you charge, ask what they regularly pay other speakers. You can accept what they offer, or ask for more depending on how busy you are. Note: You may want to accept a lower rate to get in front of your target audience.

Companies will also approach you. If a company wants you give a presentation, and it may be an opportunity for you to coach people afterwards, you can offer to speak for free. If they want you only as a one-time deal for a half day or one day workshop, charge them. Take your hourly rate and multiply it by the number of hours you will be there. Triple this rate if there will be more than two people in the room. Add in more if there are high expenses to do preparatory work.

You can also join a speaker's bureau. A speaker's bureau markets your presentations for you in exchange for a percentage of your fee. Do a search on the Internet under "Speaker's Bureau" to find out more.

B. Speaking: Via Teleclasses

Estimated Time To Get It Up And Running: 30 To 90 Days

Estimated Time To Make Money From It: 90 To 360 Days

Approximate Cost: $20 To $1,000 Per Year. (Cost includes your teleclass training [very important!] and will vary depending on the number of teleclasses you give each year.)

A teleclass is similar to a live presentation except that it is given by telephone. The difference is the callers are learning with their ears versus their eyes. At a scheduled time, the people attending your teleclass call a telephone number and they are connected with you and other callers. You greet everyone and your teleclass begins.

A teleclass is a great way to disseminate information to a lot of people at one time. You can speak for one or several hours. Your teleclass can span over one or several weeks. A good guideline regarding duration is, "What do I want to say and how long do I need to say it?"

1. Why Lead A Teleclass?

- You have access to potential clients from the comfort and privacy of your office or home. There is no additional travel time required to get to and from another physical location. All that is needed is a telephone.
- You have access to people who can refer you to potential clients.
- You build credibility with potential clients.
- You deepen relationships with existing clients.
- You reduce your marketing budget. There are no expenditures for rent, parking, food, gas, etc. The overall costs are extremely low.
- You get known for being an expert.
- You have an avenue to test new material.
- You will be able to reach many people from all over the world at one time.
- You will be to speak to people who want to hear what you have to say because they have taken time from their busy day to hear you.

- You will get more participation. People who attend a live lecture are not used to speaking up or raising their hand in a room full of strangers. People may feel more comfortable participating by telephone because using the phone is something they do on a regular basis.
- You have the opportunity to find out if what you are saying makes sense. If people participate and ask a lot of questions, your teleclass is probably a winner. If people hang up, are silent, or resist what you are saying, your topic or audience may be off the mark.

2. Teleclass Outline Sample

In addition to career coaching, I also am a mentor coach. As a result of hearing many coaches tell me that they wanted to be a full-time coach, but they were not sure if it was possible, I created a teleclass to address their concerns.

I started with an outline of what I wanted to cover. Having an outline is important because it details what you will be speaking about. It gives the reader an idea of the topic you will be discussing and what they will gain as a result of taking your teleclass. It gives you a method for flushing out ideas and crafting the content for your teleclass. Here's a copy of the outline I created:

SIX STEPS TO BECOMING A FULL-TIME COACH

Sooner or later you will get to a point when you will want to do what you love—coaching full-time. There are many decisions to make, and things to watch out for, such as how you will handle the transition while earning enough money to support yourself.

In This Lively And Informative One-Hour Teleclass You Will Learn:

- How to decide if NOW is the right time to coach full-time.
- The five critical elements you need for your transition plan.
- The top three things you need to create a work environment that supports your new role.
- The key players you need to ensure your survival.

Note: My bio, which I include with the outline, can be found in the "Speaking Outline Sample" section of this book.

Coaching Assignment #16

Create a teleclass outline and bio. Make sure your teleclass addresses and solves a problem your target audience is experiencing.

3. How To Promote And Make Money From Teleclasses

To charge or not to charge for a teleclass? I hear this question a lot. My answer is; it depends. If you want a lot of people to come, or are testing out the topic, give it away for free. If you don't mind having fewer people in the beginning, and want the money, charge for it. You may consider doing an initial teleclass for free, and then, as its popularity grows, you can charge for it. Also, you can create an introductory teleclass that is free, but one that leads in to a four-week teleclass for which you get paid. It's up to you. To determine what to charge, look at what others in your area of expertise are doing. If they are not doing teleclasses, test a price until you find one that hits. The registration numbers will tell you what price works and does not work.

If your teleclasses are free, it's because you want to meet potential clients. Make it easy for them to reach you after your teleclasses are over. Provide your contact information at the beginning and end of each teleclass. Add the names of people who register to your mailing list. (With their permission, of course.) Send notes after every teleclass, and include an offer for a complimentary or discounted initial call or meeting with you. Present discounts or invitations to other things you are doing and/or promoting in your coaching practice. You do not want to overwhelm them with e-mail, and you can build a good impression if you offer something of value on a regular basis.

For those who cannot make your teleclass when it is scheduled, you can still serve this market. Record your teleclasses and turn them into real audio/MP3 files that can be downloaded and sold from your web site. Or turn them into audiocassettes or CDs that can be sold from your web site and/or at the back of the room when you give live presentations.

To promote your teleclass, locate some of web sites that list teleclasses. These sites are a worthwhile investment because they give you a phone number (or a bridge number) to use for your teleclass and also do a lot of the marketing for you. Many of these sites require training and an upfront payment before you can list your teleclass, but the requirements are doable and the costs are low.

If you do not want to go though the process of getting trained or paying to list your teleclasses, promote them yourself. Create a separate page on your web site for your teleclasses, send potential and current clients upcoming dates, or use your e-newsletter to spread the word to subscribers. Get a bridge number and you are ready to go.

Coaching Assignment #17

Pick a date for your teleclass, list your teleclass or rent a bridge number. (Use the resources at the back of this book to assist you.) Tell everyone you know.

3-3: Networking As A Marketing Strategy

Estimated Time To Get It Up And Running: 30 To 60 Days

Estimated Time To Make Money From It: 60 To 270 Days

Approximate Cost: $0 To $1,000 Per Year. (Biggest costs come from annual fees to join groups and/or associations in addition to monthly meeting fees.)

Networking is an interesting marketing strategy because it involves the most face-to-face requirement of your time. The basic premise is that you go to places where people meet and talk to them. It can be intimating because you are putting yourself in a situation where you are open to rejection. It's effective because you are giving potential clients the opportunity to get to know you. Your face, your presence, and what you do as a coach become familiar over time.

There's a saying in the advertising business to the effect that people do not buy a product or service until they have seen it advertised seven or more times. The same principle holds true for networking. The more networking functions you attend on a regular basis, the more recognized you become.

Networking is about building relationships. You make the effort to get to know people and in turn, they make the effort to get to know you. This "know-ness" can bring in clients. Networking will not bring in immediate sales. (If this is your goal, you will be unsuccessful, and you will return to your home or office disappointed.) You may not get a new coaching client after each event, but if you continue to plug away, and build relationships, you will see results.

A. Why Networking?

Networking is powerful. It can open doors that normally would be shut. If you are not good at networking today, you can become good at it tomorrow. Consider it another piece of your coach training.

The Benefits Of Networking:

- You gain access to other successful people who also want to expand their businesses.
- You obtain referrals that can turn into new clients.
- You find out what is going on; you get to hear about opportunities and trends before other people.

B. How To Network

- Have a plan. Ask yourself these questions before you go: Will your target audience be attending? How many people do you want to meet at a particular meeting or event? Do you have ideas or business leads to share with these people? How do you want to become known by the people who can either purchase your coaching services or those who can refer coaching clients to you? The more specific you are, the greater chances of your success.
- Prepare, rehearse, and know your 30-second introduction well. This will be your ice-breaker. Your 30-second introduction needs to be clear and make sense to those who know what coaching is and those who do not.
- Use networking as a method for gathering information. Talk to people about your services. Gauge their reaction. If they change the subject, look at you strangely, or look away, then your description may be off. If they say, "Tell me more" or "That's interesting," you are probably describing what you do well. I started out telling people that I help executives find their dream careers and I got a lot of blank stares. Today, I tell people that I work with executives who are out of work or overworked. Now they want to know more.
- Establish rapport. Find things you have in common with others. We all are more comfortable around those who are similar to us.
- Speak passionately about what you do. Enthusiasm will win over even the most skeptical person. At the same time, if you see that someone does not want to talk to you, respect this, and move on.
- Do not spend too much time talking with one person. Spend 5-10 minutes per person. Initially, you want to meet as many people as possible. At subsequent meetings, you can spend more time with people.

- Listen well and maintain eye contact. Ask open-ended questions. This shows that you are interested. Do not interrupt the other person when they are speaking.

- Offer to help. Use phrases like, "What can I do for you?" "How can I help you?" "I have something or someone that may solve your problem. Would you like me to send it to you?" The best way to get referrals is to give them first.

- Look for people who not only want coaching but those who can also help you get clients. While not everyone is in the market for a coach, they may know someone who is.

- When someone tells you about a problem they are having that you solve as a coach, ask "Do you want to address this now?" If they say yes, they are a potential client. If they say no, they may or may not become a client over time. This question is very powerful because you find out if someone has client potential. You save yourself time and heartache when you know that the timing is off.

- Schedule complimentary calls or follow up meetings in the moment. Playing phone tag to schedule calls wastes your time and makes you lose momentum.

- Make notes on the back of business cards so you do not forget who you met and what you discussed/promised.

- Follow up as soon as possible. Start with those who agreed to address their problems now. If someone has a problem that needs solving, you want to be the person to help solve it.

C. Where To Network

Among others, you can network in the following places:

- Associations
- Business Groups
- Coaching Conferences
- Chambers Of Commerce
- Local Coaching Chapters

- Kiwanis Clubs
- Networking Organizations
- Rotary Clubs
- Women's Groups

Seems like a long list doesn't it? So, where do you start?

You want to network with people who can either buy your services or refer business to you. This means that you put yourself in front of people who are either your target audience or know people who are. Not sure who attends a local chamber of commerce meeting? Pick up the phone and find out. Want to know when the next Rotary Club meeting is? Get on the Internet and find out. Get as much information as you can. If you like what you hear or read, make plans to go.

When you are at the event, look around. Do you like the people? Talk to a few people to make sure. Do you like the group's mission and what it stands for? Talk to someone who runs the group and hear what he/she has to say. Is there potential business on the horizon? Ask the members what they think of the group, and how it has impacted their business. If you like what you hear, make plans to go to another meeting.

After you have attended a few events and feel there is real potential for business, volunteer for a position. It is a great way to get known and obtain clients.

D. Creating A 30-Second Introduction

An important tool to have at networking functions is a 30-second introduction. The purpose of the introduction is to get people interested in talking to you further. Thirty seconds is about how long most people have to introduce themselves. And it's about the most amount of time that people who don't know you are willing to listen to you.

Here's An Example Of How I Introduce Myself:

My name is Deborah Brown-Volkman, and I am the president of Surpass Your Dreams, a successful career and mentor coaching company based on Long Island, NY. We work with senior executives, vice presidents, and managers who are out of work or overworked. We also work with coaches who want to start and build profitable coaching practices.

<u>Here's How I Created It:</u>

I started with my name, my company names, what we do, and where we are located. (I could have added that we began in 1998 to add more credibility. Then I went into who we help specifically. My goal was to make that clear, and to entice the listener to ask me questions.

<u>Coaching Assignment #18</u>

Create your introduction and start using it. You can tell if your 30-second pitch is compelling because people will say, "I'm the person you described" or "I know someone who is the person you described." This is where your hard work to identify a target market will pay off. If your 30-second introduction is too fluffy, people will look away, say nothing, or change the subject.

E. Volunteering Your Time

To be a successful networker, you must get involved. This means volunteering your time to serve on boards and committees. Yes, this requires a commitment of your time. But what worthwhile endeavor does not take time?

Volunteering means joining an established group or starting one of your own. I attend many networking functions in search of executives who want career coaching. I also started a coaches group so I could network with other coaches who are also my target audience. This group is called The United Coaching Associates (http://www.unitedcoachingassociates.com). By leading this group, I have met coaches who have become my friends as well as coaches who have hired me to help build their practices.

Here's what I tell people when they ask me how I find the time to run a coaching group in addition to running a full-time coaching practice:

"I used to be a person who hid behind my computer and believed that this was the way I was going to grow my coaching practice. Was I ever wrong! Want to get? Give. This is something I fought my whole life until I got tired of fighting. Leading the United Coaching Associates has changed my life. I have friends, access to resources, and have learned things that I never would have dreamt possible. Get involved. Get out there. Even if you think you don't have time. Not only will you feel more confident and comfortable with your offering as a coach, but you will be part of something that you can contribute to. Getting involved can change your life."

What Volunteering Can Give You

Volunteering allows you to contribute as well as get something in return. Your time is precious. The time you spend volunteering could be spent on other things. So why do it?

- You feel a part of something bigger than yourself.
- You get to help shape the direction and success of an organization.
- You have access to the top people in the organization.
- You get to learn more about yourself.
- You get known as a leader.
- The number of people you know expands. Sometimes saying you know someone who also knows the person you are speaking with may open doors that may not have opened without this connection.

Coaching Assignment #19

Identify five key places to network in your area. (Use the resources at the back of this book to assist you.) Contact them. Ask them about the demographics and open volunteer positions. Find out their schedule for the next couple of months. Mark these dates on your calendar so you do not forget.

Step 4: Learn How To Sell

Estimated Time To Learn: 90 To 360 Days

Approximate Cost: $15 To $2,500 To Learn. (Biggest costs are books, seminars, and coaching to learn.)

Selling can be tough. Between learning how to coach, making a living as a coach, and overcoming your personal opinions about what selling is, selling can be both confusing and overwhelming. Selling can also be easy and effortless.

Fear of selling is very common in the coaching profession. Most coaches came from different careers where they were not responsible for asking customers for their business. (This task was left to someone else.) Now you are responsible for growing a coaching practice, and this means you are also responsible for selling. There are many things to learn, and they are learnable.

You cannot make money as a coach unless you ask potential clients for their business. This does not mean that you have to be pushy. It means being yourself. It's telling clients what you can do for them, and asking whether they are interested. If they say yes, you sign them up. If they say no, you thank them for their time. It can be this simple. Going through this process may be scary at first, but the conviction that you are doing what you love for a living, and getting paid for it at the same time, is a great motivator to get over your concerns.

Where Coaches Get Stuck

If selling is so learnable, why does it seem so hard? Why do coaches get stuck? Here are some explanations:

- You do not believe in yourself, your services, or you lack confidence.
- You don't have a clear target audience or lack a program.
- You are not filling a need or solving a problem.
- You are serving a market where you fulfill a need but the market will not fill your bank account.

- You are disorganized.
- You have personal problems that are affecting your coaching practice.
- You are not taking care of yourself mentally and/or physically.
- You are coaching because you need the money.
- You worry about being pushy, and as a result, you do not push at all.
- You don't end a complimentary call or meeting with "I would love to work with you. What is standing in the way of you saying YES right now?" You end a complimentary call with "If you are interested, please get back to me and let me know."
- You are afraid of success or failure.
- You are afraid of being rejected.
- You are afraid of the selling process.
- You do not value your services and are giving too much away for free.
- You do not compete on price or you sell your coaching too cheap.
- You talk too much during complimentary calls or initial meetings. A good speaking ratio for the first meeting is 80% potential client, 20% you.
- You try to force prospective clients to sign up for your coaching programs, and you go in for the quick sale.
- You are discouraged. You let outside circumstances and current events stop you.
- You do not ask for referrals.
- You do not have enough support.
- You have not hired an experienced coach who can show you the way.

Notice which ones are currently giving you the most trouble. Circle them and discuss them with your coach.

Six Key Elements Of Every Sale

There are key elements in every sale. Cover them successfully and you will gain a new client. Leave one or more out, and you will not. The elements are:

1. The prospective client's needs have been identified. You are clear what the problems are and have fully conveyed that you can help solve them.
2. The prospective client believes you have the right background and credentials.
3. The prospective client and you have built a solid rapport.
4. The prospective client objections have been handled.
5. The prospective client has a budget for coaching and is ready to buy now.
6. The perspective client hires you.

Make sure that all of these elements are addressed in your complimentary call and/or initial meeting with potential clients. If they are not, schedule a follow-up call to do so.

Coaching Assignment #20

Think about meetings or calls with prospective clients that resulted in a sale. Think about meetings or calls with prospective clients that did not. For this assignment, pick one person from each category. Answer the following set of questions either in this book or on a separate piece of paper.

A Potential Client Who **DID NOT** Become A Client

1. Were the prospective client's needs identified? Did you convey how you could help solve their problems? If no, then why not? What was missing? What would you do differently going forward?

2. Was the prospective client ready to buy now? If no, then why not?

3. Did you have the right background and credentials? Did you communicate this effectively upfront? If no, then why not? What was missing? What would you do differently going forward?

4. Were objections handled properly? Do you know why the prospective client did not proceed? What was missing? What would you do differently going forward?

5. Was a solid rapport built? If no, then why not? What was missing? What would you do differently going forward?

6. Did you close the sale? Did you ask for their business with power and confidence? If no, then why not? What was missing? What would you do differently going forward?

A Potential Client Who **DID** Became A Client

1. Were the prospective client's needs identified? If yes, how were you able to convey that you could help solve their problems? Why do you believe you were successful? What will you keep and incorporate going forward?

2. Was the prospective client ready to buy now? If yes, how did you find out?

3. Did you have the right background and credentials? Were you able to communicate this effectively? If yes, why do you believe you were successful? What will you keep and incorporate going forward?

4. Were objections handled? Did you answer all questions well? If yes, why do you believe you were successful? What will you keep and incorporate going forward?

5. Was a solid rapport built? If yes, why do you believe you were successful? What will you keep and incorporate going forward?

6. Did you close the sale? If yes, why do you believe you were successful? What will you keep and incorporate going forward?

What did you learn from this assignment? Discuss obstacles and successes with your coach.

How To Sell

Want to be successful at selling? Visualize your success beforehand. Visualize what you are doing, what you are saying, and what potential clients are doing and saying? Know the results you want in advance, and you will get the paying clients you are looking for. Here are some tips to get ready:

- Know your objective. Do you want a client or another call or appointment? Depending on the nature of the sale, an individual client could hire you after only one conversation and/or a corporate client may need a few meetings before making a decision. Know your sales cycle and respect it.

- Convey what you do and what you charge clearly. Speak in terms of benefits, not features. Speak with confidence and power.

- Establish your credibility and expertise upfront. Tell a potential client about your qualifications early in the conversation.

- Know what objections you may get, and have a response for all of them to avoid being thrown off balance when you hear them. Address and handle objections in the moment. Note: If you cannot do so (this happens a lot in the beginning), you can follow up at a later date with an answer.

- Be familiar with the type of problems the people who call you have.

- Get potential clients to open up and talk to you. Ask open-ended questions, acknowledge them for their accomplishments, and the courage it took to come to you. Be sincere.

- Have potential clients see new possibilities. Use stories to illustrate your successes or that of your clients (no real names, please.) Stories are a great way to get your points across in an interesting and relevant way.

- Listen well. Do not interrupt potential clients when they are speaking. Paraphrase what you have heard to get feedback to determine if you are correct.

- Be a coach. Know the techniques of your craft. This is where training, knowledge, and the benefits of attending relevant conferences will be put to best use.

- Be a problem-solver, not someone who wants to rush the sales process. (Be careful not to solve problems during the sales conversation. That's the coach's job, not the salesperson's job.)

- Be able to convey what other coaches in your field of expertise do. Be ready to say what makes you comparable in skill, yet different in focus or technique.

- Ask potential clients when they plan to on make a decision and if they are interviewing other coaches. Ask what their budget is for coaching. These are fair questions, and it shows that you want their business.

- Take the yeses gracefully and the no's just as well. Thank potential clients either way.

- Request coaching so you can become a more effective seller.

> **Coaching Tip:** To cold call or not to cold call? This is a question I get a lot. My answer is cold calling is tough. Some coaches say it works, while others swear it's a waste of time. When you are cold calling someone, you are disturbing the person you are calling. However, if you decide to use this strategy, open with your 30-second introduction, and ask open-ended questions until the other person softens or hangs up. Cold calling is a numbers game. Sooner or later, you will find someone who will talk to you. Keep track of how many calls you make and how long it takes to find someone who is a potential client. Assess whether this is the best use of your time.

How To Win At Complimentary Calls And/Or Initial Meetings

Complimentary calls and/or initial meetings with potential clients are important. Prospective clients are assessing whether you can help them. You are evaluating whether you want them as a client. It's a time to connect and determine if there is a fit between the two of you.

It's also NOT a time to coach. Ask open-ended questions. Get all the details you want. Empathize with what potential clients are going through, but do not coach them. They'll feel like they have their "answer" and will not hire you.

Your goal is to establish credibility, find out what the potential client needs, and explain that your program is what can help solve their problems. Bring in success stories to show that your program and coaching works. Give testimonials. Ask open end questions. Just stay away from actual coaching.

I speak from experience. When I began giving complimentary calls, I would impress potential clients with my wisdom and experience. Thirty minutes later they felt like a new person. They felt better, had direction, and believed they could fix what was broken on their own. This is another reason I created my program. So I could talk about how I would help them versus outright helping them. Now, I assess where potential clients are, and I run through how my program can be their possible solution. It is a different conversation, one that does not give answers, but leaves them wanting more.

Questions To Ask At Complimentary Calls And/Or Initial Meetings

Great complimentary calls and/or initial meetings start with great questions. Here are a few that you can use to get potential clients to open up and discuss what they want.

- What is the one thing that you don't currently have in your life/career/business that would make a huge difference to you?
- How would your life/career/business be different if you had this?
- How would having it affect the significant people in your life?
- How long have you wanted this?
- What stops you from getting it?
- Are you willing to do the work now to get it?
- What else do you want?
- How do you believe a coach can help you reach your goals?

How To Handle Objections

If you get an objection, it's not always bad news. Your goal is to respond, not react. Do not take objections personally. Repeat what a potential client has said to you, express your understanding, and ask permission to probe further, to find out why. Objections are a way that potential clients convey that they need more information first before they hire you.

Objection can also indicate that potential clients do not feel "comfortable" with you. They might not believe that you can help them. You may not have uncovered their problems/needs fully, assessed whether they were ready to buy now, or pushed too soon. Here are some common objections and ways to overcome them:

<u>1) What The Client Says:</u> "I don't have money."

Translation: "I do not see the value in what you offer." "I do not believe you can help me."

What To Do: Tell potential clients that you understand their situation and request permission to address their concern. Handle the objection first by providing numbers.

1) Ask potential clients how much their time is worth (let's say $40 an hour.) Then ask how many hours they spend worrying about their problem. (let's say 20 hours a week.) Twenty hours times $40 is $800 a week or $2,400 a month. If your coaching fee is less than that, say so. If it's more, raise the number of how much their time is worth in this calculation.

2) Ask potential clients what it would be worth to them if they did not have their problems anymore. If your coaching fee is less than that, tell them this. If it's more, raise the numbers in this calculation.

3) Show the client how much they would save by hiring you. If they have a problem that is costing them $10,000 a month and your monthly coaching fee is $2,000 a month, that's an $8,000 savings.

4) Tell a story about a client in a similar situation who had the same reservations and is grateful that they did not let money stand in their way. Try to be specific about what their problem was and the specific solution their investment bought them. Make the example relevant to the situation.

5) If you want to work with the client, ask how much they would be willing to pay you. If the number is acceptable to you, take it. If not, negotiate another number.

6) Move away from money and ask if money is the real issue or is it something else they would be willing to discuss with you. See if you can resolve what their real concerns are.

2) **What The Client Says:** "I do not have time for coaching." or "I'm very busy."

Translation: "I do not think what you are offering will work." "I do not want to do the work."

What To Do: Tell potential clients that you understand their situation and request permission to address their concern.

1) Ask potential clients where else time holds them back.

2) Ask potential clients to restate the problem and tell you what their lives would be like if they had the solution already.

3) Ask potential clients how much time they spend worrying about their problem. Have them tell you what they would do with this time once their problem was solved.

4) Tell potential clients that a coach can help them make room for their goal.

5) Tell a story about a client in a similar situation (no real names!) who had the same reservation and is grateful that they set aside time to work with you. Try to be specific what their problem was and the specific solution their time investment gave them. Make the example relevant to the situation.

3) What The Client Says: "I will get back to you."

Translation: "I do not see the value in what you offer." "I do not believe you can help me."

What To Do: Ask potential clients if they have unanswered questions. If they do, answer them. If they are still not ready to make a decision, respect that. Make an appointment to have a follow-up conversation if they are open to it. Most of the time, when potential clients say they will get back to you, at the time they say it, they mean it, and they just get busy. If potential clients do not schedule follow up calls with you, then you know they are not interested. The hope factor is taken away, and you can concentrate on other things.

4) What The Client Says: "I have to speak to my husband or wife first."

Translation: "I am not comfortable making a decision yet." "I either do not have all the facts, or I do not believe you can help solve my problem." "I do not see the value in what you offer."

What To Do: Make sure all the client's questions have been answered. Then, with their permission, ask potential clients what they CAN commit to right now. Can they schedule tentative coaching dates and confirm this after they speak with their spouse? Can they give you their contact information? Making small commitments is a step in the right direction.

Once all objections have been addressed, ask for the sale again. Do not speak once you ask potential clients for their business even if you are tempted to do so. Let them speak first. Watch out that you do not get caught up in the trap of asking for their business and then talking so much afterwards that they will not be able to answer you. Do not let your nervousness get in the way.

Coaching Tip: Expect no's. It takes a lot of no's to get to yes.

Coaching Assignment #21

Make a list of all the objections you have been hearing or you think you will hear from potential clients. Write them down along with your answers.

How To Follow Up With Prospects

Just because potential clients do not say yes today does not mean they will not say yes tomorrow. For every client that hired me after one conversation, there was another who needed more time to think about it. One recent client said that she waited four years to hire me as her coach. She saw me at a networking meeting four years earlier and indicated that I made an impression on her, but was not ready to work with me at that time. So, you never know.

I hear from many coaches "How long do I wait to call a prospect back?" or "What's the best way to follow up with someone I have met at a networking function or had a complimentary call with?"

Here are some tips on what to do:

- Organize a good follow-up system whether it is paper or electronic. Record everything a prospect tells you and their time frame for making a decision. Note who you need to contact and when. Follow up when you say you will, whether you made the promise to the prospect or yourself.
- If possible, schedule another appointment after every conversation. This way the decision is not left open. It is a good way to discover a prospect's

intentions. If they schedule another call with you, that shows they are interested. If not, they are not. (Right now.)

- Send an e-mail or call noncommittal prospects once every two weeks, but do not be a pest. Contact them with information they can use such as an article that would be relevant to them, or a web site that would be useful.

- Know when to give up. If a prospect does not return your e-mail or phone calls, take that as a sign that they are not interested. Keep them on your mailing list.

- When a prospect says they are not interested, respect their decision. Ask them if you may contact them in the future. If they say yes, do so. If they say no, take them off your contact list.

After The Sale

Once a client says, "Yes!" schedule your first coaching call (or meeting), within a day or two. Send the client an agreement that spells out the terms of the coaching relationship, and includes your coaching fee. Ask for your client's signature on the contract. Make arrangements for payment, get their credit card number, or ask them to write you a check. (If they are mailing the check, ask for a date when you will be receiving it.)

You are helping your clients start a new chapter in their lives, and some may resist the process. When clients say yes, they are making a positive decision. Later on, some clients experience what's called "Buyer's Remorse"—I shouldn't have, I can't, I don't wanna, etc. This is a very powerful, negative emotion that may keep your clients from following through with their commitment. Your job is to help them get past this.

Before you end the conversation, ask them if there is anything they can think of that would cause them to not to go forward. They will probably say no. Ask them to commit to and trust the process even if they experiences fear later on. If they encounter buyer's remorse, they'll remember that they gave their word to their coach. This will help to keep them engaged in the coaching relationship.

Bonus Step: Working With The Press

Estimated Time To Get It Up And Running: 60 To 90 Days

Estimated Time To Make Money From It: 90 To 360 Days

Approximate Cost: $0 To $5,000 Per Year. (Biggest costs come from using outside companies for press release distribution, reporter names, and leads for stories that reporters are working on.)

Getting coverage in top newspapers and magazines is not as hard as you may believe. There are thousands of newspapers and magazines in the world today. Each one has to come up with news on a regular basis, sometimes monthly, weekly, and, in many cases, daily.

Reporters and editors are regular people. They have a job to do. Their job is to cover the news and find people who can make their job easier. They need you. They need your stories. The best thing about the news is it's not about who you know. It's about what you have to say.

You know more about what you do than anyone else. And if what you do is interesting (it is!), people will want to know about it.

Why The Press Is Important

- You get your name and opinions out into the world. You discover that people are interested in you and what you think.
- It's an excellent medium for building credibility. The printed word from a third party gives you more credibility that when the same words come out of your mouth. Even though the media get criticized for how they obtain the news, they are the most respected source for information.
- It is much cheaper than advertising. The cost is your time spent writing press releases and having interviews with reporters.

- Reprints of stories in which you have been featured or quoted will impress potential and current clients. My clients like to forward stories I have been quoted in to their family and friends. They like to say, "This is my coach!"

What The Press Is Interested In

There are many things you can convey to a reporter about your coaching practice. Here are a few ideas:

- Your new practice, a new web site, or a new product or service that is getting results for your clients, a different type of coaching (humor coaching, sensitive people coaching) or a new book you have written.
- A story that is exclusive. Reporters like to be first to break new stories.
- A coaching program or service that is tied into current events. For example: after September 11, the International Coach Federation started a pro bono coaching group that coached World Trade Center survivors and their families.

Other ways to get coverage:

- Coach journalists and reporters. They may write about their experience or you. (Note: Be careful about offering free coaching to a journalist who is writing a story about you. The publication may see this as a conflict of interest.)
- Ask to have a personal profile written about you. Many newspapers will do a profile on a local business owner.
- Call a magazine or a newspaper and ask for a copy of their Editorial Calendar. An Editorial Calendar lists what they are planning to run as feature stories throughout the year. Time your news to their schedule.

Coaching Assignment #22

What about your coaching practice would the press would be interested in? Make a list of five story ideas now.

How To Write A Press Release

A press release is the main way to communicate with the press. It is a standard document that conveys all the information a reporter needs to determine if what you have to say is newsworthy. Unless you have a groundbreaking or exclusive story, most reporters will not talk to you unless they see your press release first.

Format Of A Press Release:

- FOR IMMEDIATE RELEASE (Standard in all releases)
- HEADLINE (Make it catchy!)
- CONTACT INFORMATION (Contact Person, Company Name, Telephone Number, E-mail Address, Web site address)
- CITY, STATE, DATE & OPENING PARAGRAPH (should contain who, what, when, where, why)
- BODY OF RELEASE (Details, interesting facts, Use quotes when possible.)
- COMPANY HISTORY (Your company/coaching info)
- # # # (Indicates Press Release is finished)

> **Coaching Tip:** Have a page on your web site that is devoted to the press. Include past press releases, your contact information, a fact sheet about your practice, where you have been quoted before, and any other materials you want the press to have access to. This is very useful information when a reporter is deciding whether to interview you.

Press Release You Can Follow

Here's an example of a press release that I wrote. Notice how it follows the format of press release components. I did a similar release at the end of 2002 and a reporter from Long Island Business News saw it and did an exclusive story on me.

FOR IMMEDIATE RELEASE

Telephone Seminars That Make The Dream Of Becoming A Coach A Reality. Seminars Help Answer The Question: "What Should I Be Doing With My Life?"

Contact: Deborah Brown-Volkman
Email: info@surpassyourdreams.com
Web site: www.surpassyourdreams.com

(Long Island, NY—November 1, 2003) Deborah Brown-Volkman, President of Surpass Your Dreams, Inc., a career and mentor coaching company based in Long Island, NY, announces the new telephone seminar schedule for 2004. The focus of the seminars is how to live the dream of becoming a successful and profitable full-time coach.

"There is so much information available regarding how to become a coach, or how to make money at it, that it can all become confusing and overwhelming," says Deborah Brown-Volkman. "These seminars help both new and experienced coaches so they do not have to go through the process of living their dream of becoming a full-time coach alone."

Seminar Titles Include: So, You Wanna Be A Coach? Five Things You Need To Know Before You Get Started; Seven Ways To Win New Clients; and Six Steps To Becoming A Full-Time Coach.

"Coaching is getting more popular by the day because it brings fulfillment and satisfaction," says Deborah. "It fills the void and answers the question: 'Why do I feel like something is missing in my life?' and 'What should I be doing with my life?' Coaching provides something that no other profession has provided so far."

"We have the honor of saying that we are a coach," Deborah continues. "We get to bring our talents, skills, experience, and passion to our profession. We can look anyone in the eye and say that we are making a difference in the world. How many people can say that?"

Telephone seminars are a great way to gain knowledge and new ideas from the comfort of a home or office. All seminars are one hour in length and are packed with information participants can use immediately. Whether someone wants to decide whether to move into the coaching profession or how to live the dream of becoming a full-time coach, there is a seminar available that that can provide this information.

About Surpass Your Dreams:

Surpass Your Dreams, Inc. is a successful career and mentor coaching company that has been delivering a message of motivation, success, and personal fulfill-ment since 1998. We work with senior executives, vice presidents, and man-agers who are out of work or overworked. We also work with coaches who want to start and build profitable coaching practices. For more information, please contact Deborah Brown-Volkman, President, info@surpassyour-dreams.com or at www.surpassyourdreams.com/coaches.html

###

Coaching Tip: Include a letter of introduction with your press release. Include your area of expertise, that you are available to comment on other stories, and your contact information.

Coaching Tip: Coverage leads to move coverage. When you contact the press, let them know where you have been quoted before.

Coaching Assignment #23

Write a press release. Take a story idea from the last coaching assignment and use the components of a press release and my example to write your own.

Where To Send Your Press Release

In order for reporters to read your press release, they have to receive it. There are several press release distribution services that will send out your press release for you. The advantage is you give them your credit card number and release and they distribute it. The drawback is this method is expensive, and you do not get access to the names of the reporters who receive your release.

The next time you want to send out a release, you have to start from scratch, and pay again.

Another method is to use Media Directory companies that will sell you targeted lists with reporter's complete contact information and what they write about. The advantage is this saves you time and money researching the information yourself. And the names are for you to keep. The drawback is that Media Directories are expensive. Very expensive.

I decided that I did not want to spend the money building a list, so I built my own. This is how I built my list:

I went to Yahoo.com and did a search for newspapers and magazines. Since I am a career coach, I looked for reporters in business magazines and newspapers who wrote about careers. If they had a link to a web site, I visited it and collected their e-mail address. I also searched for career sites, job boards, search firms, and other sites related to getting a new job or being more effective in the current one you have. I collected more e-mail addresses.

What I could not locate on the Internet, I found in a bookstore. I sat one day with a pile high of magazines and newspapers (while eating a scone and drinking a large cup of coffee), and read and collected more names. If I could not find a name, I called the publication and asked for it. Yes, this took some time, and it was worth it. I started my database with five names and now it's in the hundreds.

As you do your research, look for reporters who write about your field of expertise. Get to know these reporters. Read stories that they have written. When you speak with reporters and you tell them you liked an article they wrote, it goes a long way.

Only include reporters on your list who are interested in receiving your press release. As a career coach, I would not send a press release to a reporter who writes about leisure activities or cooking. It sends a signal that I do not know who I am sending my release to and that I do not care. I would much rather send a release to five reporters who want it than to a thousand reporters who don't.

Coaching Assignment #24

Decide how you will to distribute your press release. Select a method and send out your press release.

> **Coaching Tip:** Reporters like e-mailed releases better than fax or mail.

> **Coaching Tip:** Put your catchy title in the header and do not send press releases as attachments. Cut and paste your releases and put them into the body of e-mails.

How To Build Great Relationships With The Press

The way to build a great relationship with the press is to become an expert they can rely on when they are in the midst of writing a story. Reporters are frequently on tight deadlines and they need to have a rolodex of good sources to contact on a consistent basis.

Reporters are looking for smart and honest experts. They know you want to be included in their stories and will oblige if you give them the best information you can.

Here are a few tips for successfully starting and building this relationship:

1. Never lie to a reporter.
2. Be friendly, upbeat, and easy to work with. Be real and authentic.
3. Be yourself. Confidence attracts.
4. Be accessible. Reporters may need to get in touch with you quickly. Return their calls immediately, even if the story they are writing about does not apply to you.
5. If you promise to send information, do so right away.

6. Become a news junkie. Know what's going on in the news and in your field so that you can tie your press release into something that is current and topical.

7. Know your topic well.

How To Successfully Handle A Press Interview

Here's the scenario. A reporter picks up your release and is interested in speaking with you. How do you deliver information successfully without wasting the reporter's time or coming across poorly? Here are some tips:

1. Everything you say is on the record unless you say otherwise.

2. Prepare. Then prepare some more. Never go into an interview without mapping out the three or four points you want to make. Prioritize them. Then boil your points down to short, interesting, quotable "sound bites." Use your coach to role-play with you.

3. Answer the reporter's questions in as few sentences as possible. Reporters take notes and cannot write as quickly as you speak. Smaller pieces of information are easier for them to digest. If they want more information, or clarity, they will tell you. Do not go on tangents. Use your knowledge of the reporter's style and what's important to his/her readers to shape how you answer questions.

4. State your message in a positive way. Negative comments turn reporters off.

5. Do not answer a question you are not fully prepared to answer. If you are not confident, ask more questions until you fully understand what the reporter is asking. If you do not know the answer, tell the reporter that. It is better to say, "I don't know" than to make something up.

6. It's okay to be nervous, but try to stay calm. The hardest part of an interview is the beginning because you are not sure what the reporter will ask you. The interview will get easier as it goes along. If you get stuck, pause, take a deep breath, and think your answer through before speaking.

7. Ask when the story is coming out. Tell the reporter that you look forward to reading it. If you can't buy the publication because it is a paid subscription, ask the reporter for a copy.

8. Thank the reporter for the interview and tell him/her that even if you're not included in this story, you are available for brainstorming in the future.

9. After the interview, send an e-mail thanking the reporter for the opportunity. Include three to five key points discussed. Do this right away. This reduces the likelihood of being misquoted, particularly if a reporter is relying only on his/her own notes.

10. A reporter may or may not use you for a story. The editor has the final say regarding what goes into the story. Do not get discouraged or take it personally. As long as you were helpful, there is a good chance that the reporter will call you again about a future story.

Coaching Assignment #25

Practice a press interview. Ask your coach to help you. The practice will increase your confidence.

Turning Press Mentions Into Paying Clients

You've spent the time and the money to create a relationship with the press, and the results have paid off: Your name is in top newspapers and magazines. How can you turn this into paying clients?

List your press mentions on your web site, in your e-newsletter, at the beginning of teleclasses, workshops, etc. Include press mentions on your bio. Send copies or reprints of publications in which you have been quoted to clients and prospective clients either by e-mail or mail.

Your name was in print and this will make an impression. Many clients became clients because they saw my name in a newspaper or magazine. It makes a difference, and is worth the time and energy it takes to get a press strategy going.

Conclusion

Did you become a coach because you wanted to share your gift with the world? Were you also tired of working in other professions that did not seem right for you? Were you tired of not having a career with purpose and meaning? Were you tired of not being paid what you were worth? Were you tired of working long hours for someone else?

Do you want to be financially independent? Do you want to be your own boss? Yes? This is what coaching can provide.

There will be challenges and obstacles as you go from "I think I want to be a coach" to "I have a full-time coaching practice." Don't let marketing be the obstacle that stops you. Do a little of what is in this book every day. Use the book as a resource to guide you. Use what you know and learn what you don't so you can make your dream of having a profitable coaching practice a reality. And don't forget to hire a coach.

Resources

1. Marketing Resources

- Web site for software to automate your practice and the creation of forms for your coaching practice: http://www.clientcompass.com or 425-822-3040

- Web site for a program to fill your practice: http://www.fillyourpractice.com/

- Web sites to list your coaching services: http://www.findacoach.com/index.html, http://www.coachvillereferral.com, or http://www.coachfederation.org/referral/index.htm

- Web site for coaching programs: http://www.coachville.com

- Web site for an inexpensive logo for your web site, business cards, and stationery: http://www.gotlogos.com/ support@GotLogos.com

- Web site for inexpensive and professional looking business cards: http://www.vistaprint.com VistaPrint USA Incorporated, 100 Hayden Avenue, Lexington, MA 02421. 781-890-8434

- Web site to become a credit card merchant: http://www.practicepaysolutions.com 800-326-9897 or 888-627-2730 info@practicepaysolutions.com

- Web site for alternative methods of accepting payments: http://www.paypal.com or http://www.quickbooks.com

- Web site to promote your coaching practice: "The Coaching Show" on www.wsRadio.com. Contact: Andrea Wylan, 858-457-7558 or awylan@san.rr.com

- 15-Point Checklist you can use to grow a profitable coaching practice. Written by Judy Feld, Master Certified Coach (MCC), and President, International Coach Federation (ICF) 2003. Send an e-mail to judy@coachnet.com with "Three R's" in the subject line.

2. Web Site Resources

- Web site for domain names: http://www.godaddy.com, http://register.com or http://www.netsol.com
- Web site hosting: http://www.innerhost.com (1-877-HOSTING)
- Web site to build your own web site: http://www.domaindirect.com help@domaindirect.com
- Service that will list your site in search engines for you: http://www.searchenginesbyhand.com/coaches
- Web sites for e-mailing lists, autoresponders, and shopping cart programs: http://www.cartville.com, http://www.professionalcartsolutions.com, http://www.quickpaypro.com, http://www.aweber.com, http://www.getresponse.com
- Free Adobe Reader: http://www.adobe.com/products/acrobat/readstep2.html
- Web site to get and create a blogger: http://www.blogger.com
- Web site that checks for broken links on your web site: http://www.elsop.com/linkscan/quickcheck.html
- Web tool to shrink the images on your web site so they are faster to load. I love this program: http://www.spinwave.com/crunchers.html
- Web site for a well-designed e-mail signature: http://www.inboxart.com Inbox Art, Inc., PO Box 224, Crownsville, MD 21032. info@inboxart.com
- Web and e-mail marketer: http://www.peer360.com Peer360, Inc., 475 Central Avenue, Suite 403 St. Petersburg, FL 33701. 727-898-1119. info@peer360.com
- Talented Web Site Designer http://www.tagonline.com 248 Lorraine Ave, 2nd Floor, Upper Montclair, NJ 07043 973-783-5583 Fax: 973-783-5334 sales@tagonline.com Ask for Amy.

3. E-Newsletter Resources

- Web site to promote your e-newsletter: http://www.newsletterpromote.com/ 16 SenatorWalk, London, England, SE28 0EH. info@newsletterpromote.com or sales@newsletterpromote.com 44 (0) 870-744-2633

- Web site to manage your e-newsletter: http://www.ezinemanager.com (support@ezinemanager.com), http://fortunecity.roving.com/home.jsp (Constant Contact-support@roving.com), or http://www.ezezine.com/
- Web site for content for your e-newsletter: http://www.topten.org
- Web site for top e-zine directories to list your e-newsletter: http://ezines.nettop20.com/
- Web site for a monthly service that allows coaches to publish a beautiful, content-rich e-newsletter with little effort at an affordable price. Dina Silver, CPCC, Founder, Pegasus Coaching Group, Publisher, Monthly Reflections, 310-393-8082, dina@pegasuscoachinggroup.com http://www.monthlyreflections.com
- Web site that allows you in less than an hour to create a professionally written, visually appealing, high-quality newsletter without writing a word. Print, HTML, PDF and text versions are available. http://www.theprofessionalnotes.com
- Web site that provides customized newsletters for coaches: http://www.coachingmatters.com/ or r_krakoff@laguna.com.mx or 1-888-800-NEWS

4. Article Resources

- Web site that formats your articles into plain text and 65 characters per line so they are easily read by different e-mail users: http://www.formatit.com/
- Web site that lists article directories you can submit your articles to: http://www.marketing-seek.com/dcd/Article_Directories/
- Web site for a list of magazines by subject: http://dir.yahoo.com/News_and_Media/Magazines/
- Web site for a list of newspapers by region: http://dir.yahoo.com/News_and_Media/Newspapers/
- Web site for on-line newspapers: http://www.onlinenewspapers.com/
- Web site for newspaper web sites around the world: http://www.newspaperlinks.com
- Web site and e-book that shows you how to get paid for your articles: http://www.ilovetowrite.com Blue Moon Communications, 6 Basset Place, Bear, Delaware 19701. Ilovetowrite@Ilovetowrite.com

5. E-Book Resources

- Web site that turn your e-book into a PDF format: http://www.neevia.com/express/
- Web sites to create and compile your e-book: http://www.e-ditor.com/ or http://superwin.com/super.htm
- Web site for e-book templates: http://www.web-source.net/ebookstarter/ebooktemplates.htm
- Web sites for e-book covers: http://www.killercovers.com or http://www.ecovergenerator.com/
- Web site for e-book and software resources: http://www.ebooksnbytes.com/
- Web site that lists e-book directories to submit your e-book to: http://www.ebooksubmit.com/ebookdirectories.html
- Web site that offers e-book submission promotion services: http://www.ebooksubmit.com/
- Web site that reviews e-books: http://www.forewordreviews.com Contact Alex Moore, Review Editor at reviews@forewordmagazine.com and http://www.ebook-reviews.net/
- Web site that catalogs e-books for libraries: http://www.netlibrary.com
- Seller and publisher of e-books: http://www.BookLocker.com
- E-books & Documents section on amazon.com: http://www.amazon.com/exec/obidos/tg/browse/-/551440/002-9219884-3631236
- Turn your e-book into a printed booklet: Paulette@tipsbooklets.com or http://www.tipsbooklets.com
- Turn you e-book into a book: Judy Cullins helps coaches take book and e-book ideas and make them real. Judy@bookcoaching.com, 619-466-0622 or http://www.bookcoaching.com

6. Speaking and Networking Resources

- Rachel Spaulding, Public Speaking Coach: http://www.live-it-coach.com Rachel@live-it-coach.com 718-275-2074
- Toastmasters: http://www.toastmasters.org
- Speaker's University: http://www.schrift.com

- Speaker Net News—weekly resource for the professional speaking community: http://www.speakernetnews.com
- National Speakers Association: http://www.nsaspeaker.org/
- Free articles on public speaking: http://www.public-speaking.org/
- Listing of Associations: http://www.ipl.org/div/aon/
- Listing of Chamber Of Commerce's: http://www.uschamber.com/default
- Listing of Rotary Clubs: http://www.rotary.org/
- Listing of Kiwanis Clubs: http://www.kiwanis.org/
- Listing of Colleges and Universities: http://dir.yahoo.com/Education/Higher_Education/Colleges_and_Univ ersities/By_Region/Countries/
- Listing of Economic Development Agencies: http://www.ecodevdirectory.com/
- Listing of Hospitals: http://adams.mgh.harvard.edu/hospitalwebusa.html
- Listing of Libraries: http://dir.yahoo.com/Reference/Libraries/
- Le Tip (Business Leads Organization): http://www.letip.com/
- BNI (The World's Largest Referral Organization): http://www.bni.com

7. Teleclass Resources

- Web site to take teleclasses, list teleclasses, as well as get trained as a Teleclass Leader: http://www.teleclassinternational.com
- Web site for bridge rentals: http://www.telephonebridgeservices.com
- Web site to tape your teleclasses or live events so they can be turned into downloadable audio files or audiocassettes/CDs: http://www.audiostrategies.com
- Web site for an Audio Podium: http://www.healthyrelating.com/audiopodium.html
- Free Real Audio Player: http://www.real.com/realoneplayer.html?pp=home&src=013103 realhome_1_3
- Transcription service. You talk, they write: http://www.type4you.com or 877-Type-4-You (877-897-3496).

8. Selling Resources

- Jeffery Gitomer—well known selling guru: http://www.gitomer.com
- Contact Management: http://www.clientcompass.com or 425-822-3040

9. Press Resources

- Web site for a free template to create your press releases:
  http://www.coachville.com/cvmembers/pressreleasedesign/
- Web site to for a free press release distribution service:
  http://www.prweb.com/
- Web site for a list of magazines by subject:
  http://dir.yahoo.com/News_and_Media/Magazines/
- Web site for a list of newspapers by region:
  http://dir.yahoo.com/News_and_Media/Newspapers/
- Web site for on-line newspapers: http://www.onlinenewspapers.com/
- Web site for newspaper web sites around the world:
  http://www.newspaperlinks.com
- Web site for hungry PR coaches: http://www.publicityinsider.com
- Web sites to get listed as an expert as well as receive e-mail from reporters who are looking for experts for stories:
  http://www.profnet.com or http://www.prleads.com
- Web site for a free clipping service:
  http://www.icopyright.com/content_user/clipandcopy.html

10. Starting Your Practice Resources

- A Free Internet Course On How To Start A Business:
  http://www.myownbusiness.org
- Business Planning Tools, Software, Resources & Sample Business Plans to get you started: http://www.businessplans.org
- IRS information on what you need to do and think about before starting your coaching practice: http://www.irs.gov
- A Small Business Administration guide to legally structuring your coaching practice: http://www.sba.gov/library/pubs/mp-25.pdf

- Web site for medical insurance: http://www.coachfederation.org (Note: This is a member benefit.)
- Web site for professional liability insurance: http://www.certifiedcoach.org

11. Growing & Expanding Your Practice Resources

- Donna Knapp, CPA. Accounting, tax and business analytics, as well as on-line processing of QuickBooks monthly reconciliations. http://www.webreadyzone.com. (512) 328-7358 dknapp@webreadyzone.com
- Book editor and ghostwriter: Vida Jurisic la.vidabiz@sympatico.ca, 416-360-8428
- Virtual Assistant: Audrey Martorana, AccessAudrey, P.O. Box 93174, Lakeland, FL 33804-3174. 863-858-8944 AccessAudrey@worldnet.att

12. Training & Accreditation Resources

- Largest coaches portal: http://www.coachville.com
- Governing body for the coaching industry: http://www.coachfederation.org
- International Coach Federation's list of accredited coaching training programs: http://www.coachfederation.org/training/organizations.htm
- International Coach Federation list of requirements to become a certi-fied coach: http://www.coachville.com/cvmembers/certifiedcoach.html
- CoachVille's coach training program: http://www.schoolofcoaching.com/
- CoachVille's coach certification program: http://www.certifiedcoach.org
- Coach Training Alliance certified coach program: http://www.coachtrainingalliance.com

13. Coaching Conference Resources

- CoachVille Conferences: http://www.coachvilleconference.com
- International Coach Federation Conferences: http://www.coachfederation.org/conference/index.htm
- Calendar of coaching events: http://www.coachingevents.com/

14. Coaching E-Zines Resources

- 52 quick tips and insights for building and filling your coaching practice: http://www.coachingcompass.com
- Free e-zine to help you attract new clients, increase your income, and improve your personal marketing:
  http://www.willcraig.com/newsletter.html
- Listing of CoachVille coach-related and other informative e-zines:
  http://www.Ezineville.com
- CoachVille's most popular coaching e-zine:
  http://www.todayscoach.com

15. Other Coaching Resources

- Coach referrals:
  http://www.unitedcoachingassociates.com/findacoach.html
- Great Coaching Books To Read:
  http://www.surpassyourdreams.com/resource4.html
- Great Coaching Web Sites:
  http://www.surpassyourdreams.com/resource3.html
- Do you need a ZIP + 4 Code(s) for a city? Or all cities in a ZIP Code?
  http://www.usps.com/zip4/
- Want to know what time a potential or current client will be calling you?
  http://www.timeanddate.com/
- Great company for phone and headsets: http://www.hellodirect.com or 1-800-HELLO34
- Web site to shop and compare calling cards' price, minutes and more.
  http://www.callingcards.com
- Web site to send personalized coaching e-greeting cards:
  http://www.coachcards.com/
- Web site to create on-line surveys: http://www.advancedsurvey.com
- Web site to set up on-line appointments:
  http://www.appointmentquest.com
- Web site so you can receive faxes that come right into your computer. No fax machine or additional equipment is required: http://www.efax.com

About The Author

Deborah Brown-Volkman

I am the president and founder of Surpass Your Dreams, Inc., a career and mentor coaching company that has been delivering a message of motivation, success, and personal fulfillment since 1998. We work Senior Executives, Vice Presidents, and Managers who are out of work or overworked. We also work with Coaches who want to build profitable coaching practices.

Current and former clients include individuals from: JPMorganChase, Oracle Corporation, Lucent Technologies, General Motors, Procter & Gamble, Ziff Davis, IBM, American Express, EDS, Ogilvy & Mather, McCann-Erickson Worldgroup, Columbia University, New York University, Chief Executive Magazine, MSNBC, and BMW.

I am a published writer, and my articles on how to be successful in your career can be found on more than 100 web sites. I am the author of an e-book titled *Living A Life You Love! The Pathway to Personal Freedom* that can help you discover your ideal career by discovering yourself first. I write a monthly e-mail newsletter and weekly tips titled *Surpass Your Dreams* that offers practical advice and steps so Monday can be the best day of the work week.

I have been quoted as a career expert by the *Wall Street Journal*, the *New York Times*, *Smart Money Magazine*, and *New York Newsday*, as well as having been interviewed by *Entrepreneur Magazine* and *Business 2.0*. I was also a featured guest on BBC, Radio Scotland when they came to New York City to find out how people were coping in their careers since the September 11th attacks.

I am a graduate of Coach University's Coaches Program, an accredited program for business & personal coaching, and am enrolled in Coachville's Graduate School Of Coaching. I also am the president and the founder of the *United Coaching Associates*, a founding member of Coachville.com, and a member of the International Coach Federation.

Before becoming a coach, I spent twelve years managing sales and marketing programs for Fortune 500 companies and dot.coms. I received an A.A.S. degree in data processing from Queensborough Community College, a B.A. in marketing from Hofstra University, and a certificate in financial planning from New York University.

My husband Brian and I live in Long Island, NY.

For additional information, you can contact me at http://www.surpassyourdreams.com or by e-mail at info@surpassyourdreams.com

0-595-29660-2

37063672R00094

Are you frustrated with trying to grow and market your coaching practice? Do you feel like there is too much information (or too little) on how to market your practice, yet not enough direction on where to begin? Would you like quick answers and a complete resource guide in one place that makes marketing easy to apply and understand?

This book will show you how to build and market a profitable coaching practice in four easy steps. It walks you through the process of deciding who to coach and how to create a program that potential clients will pay you lots of money for. You will understand the components of creating a winning marketing strategy and learn tips and techniques to implement your plan. You will also discover how to become masterful at both marketing and selling.

"*Four Steps To Building A P*  *a clear and concise guide to niche-marketing for coac*
—Talane Miedaner, best-selling author of *Coach Yourself To Success*

"*A great book with a lot of valuable information from a master at doing what she does best.*"
—Sandy Vilas, Master Certified Coach and CEO CoachInc.com

"*This is a great book. Thorough, professional, and easy to read.*"
—Judy Feld, Master Certified Coach and President International Coach Federation (ICF) 2003

Deborah Brown-Volkman is the president of Surpass Your Dreams, Inc., a successful career and mentor coaching company, that has been delivering a message of motivation, success, and personal fulfillment since 1998.

ISBN 0-595-29660-2

51595

9 780595 296606

$15.95 U.S.
$21.95 Canada
£13.99 U.K.

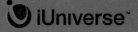 iUniverse™

www.iuniverse.com